Master Teachers

Making a Difference on the Edge of Chaos

Dexter Chapin

Rowman & Littlefield Education
Lanham • New York • Toronto • Plymouth, UK

Published in the United States of America
by Rowman & Littlefield Education
A Division of Rowman & Littlefield Publishers, Inc.
A wholly owned subsidiary of The Rowman & Littlefield Publishing Group, Inc.
4501 Forbes Boulevard, Suite 200, Lanham, Maryland 20706
www.rowmaneducation.com

Estover Road
Plymouth PL6 7PY
United Kingdom

British Library Cataloguing in Publication Information Available

Library of Congress Cataloging-in-Publication Data

Chapin, Dexter, 1944–
  Master teachers : making a difference on the edge of chaos /
Dexter Chapin.
     p. cm.
  ISBN-13: 978-1-57886-862-9 (cloth : alk. paper)
  ISBN-10: 1-57886-862-9 (cloth : alk. paper)
  ISBN-13: 978-1-57886-863-6 (pbk. : alk. paper)
  ISBN-10: 1-57886-863-7 (pbk. : alk. paper)
  ISBN-13: 978-1-57886-894-0 (electronic)
  ISBN-10: 1-57886-894-7 (electronic)
  1. Effective teaching. 2. Teachers—Professional relationships. I. Title.
  LB1025.3.C415 2009
  371.102—dc22   2008021951

⊗™ The paper used in this publication meets the minimum requirements
of American National Standard for Information Sciences—Permanence of
Paper for Printed Library Materials, ANSI/NISO Z39.48-1992.
Manufactured in the United States of America.

Very early in my life, Bill Amos introduced me to complex, adaptive systems. He did not call them that, but that's what they were. Later I was taught by Dan Huden, Barry Clemson, and Gregory Bateson, each of whom changed my life. But this book is for Karen, who gave me time to learn.

Contents

Introduction

This is a book primarily about teachers and the dynamics of the classroom. It is written because it seems to me that the No Child Left Behind legislation has impoverished the national discourse about education and teaching. That law, by legitimizing a stark, one-size-fits-all, industrial model of education, has denied the inherent complexity and richness of what teachers do. This book is about teaching as a personal connection between the teacher and the students in the classroom.

This book is not a report of the "state of education." There are no tables, no statistics, and no exhaustive surveys. Statistics and surveys certainly have their place, but not here. This is a report of observations made over the course of thirty-five years of experience in eighth to twelfth grades at an embarrassing number of public, community, and independent schools. I started off as a youngster, with maybe a little bit of promise if I survived, and, with the help of hundreds of teachers, have magically been transformed into one of the senior faculty. Along the way, I've talked to, and listened to, teachers, good and bad, effective and ineffective, about who they are, what they do, and why they do it that way. It has been a fascinating conversation. This book is an effort to report on what was said.

Much of what I report is well known to master teachers. However, Peter Drucker points out that "teaching is the only major occupation of man for which we have not yet developed tools that make an average person capable of competence and performance. In teaching we rely on the 'naturals'; the ones who somehow know how to teach."[1] Master teachers certainly know how to teach. Maybe some of it comes naturally, but some of it is clearly learned. First-year teachers are rarely master teachers. This book is about that part of being a master teacher that can be learned.

This is not a book of recipes. There is no yellow brick road to teaching success. The outcome of any recipe is, within narrow limits, specified. As will be seen, excellent teaching is an extraordinarily complex, adaptive enterprise undertaken at the edge of chaos where creativity and invention are maximized. Every master teacher teaches in his own inimitable style. No recipe can possibly be successful; it cannot begin to produce the varieties of excellent teaching.

Really excellent teaching may occur at the edge of chaos but is not chaotic. While the details are always different, there are patterns common to being a master teacher. The patterns connect the components of effective teaching in ways that give meaning and stability to the classroom. This book is an exploration of those patterns that allow master teachers to get up morning after morning and make a genuine, positive difference in students' lives.

The book is organized into sections starting with questions of who teaches, why they teach, and how they become teachers. The middle sections focus on what and how to teach. The fourth and fifth sections look at how to manage the process of teaching, and how to survive being a teacher. The final section is about making a difference outside of the classroom.

This is not a coldly dispassionate report. I am a teacher. I cannot imagine earning a living in any other fashion. I admire people who do other things for a living. I just do not want to be them even when I covet their paychecks. I've tried other careers, but teaching allows me to get up in the morning and play all day.

NOTE

1. "Teachers and Teacher Quotes." Retrieved January 15, 2008, from http://thinkexist.com/quotations/teachers_and_teaching/3.html.

CHAPTER 1

Becoming a Teacher

THE DIFFERENCES BETWEEN PARENTS AND TEACHERS

Before we get started, there is an important distinction that has to be made. The most important and influential teacher in a student's life is the parent. It is a short step from that fact to the idea that teachers are just doing what parents do, only they get paid for it. Again, it is a short step from that idea to a second idea, that teachers can and should take on more and more of the kinds of education and responsibilities that have traditionally been the parents' bailiwick. Certainly, schools, and teachers, have been given increasingly broader mandates to meet a wide range of student needs. But parents and teachers are different, very different, and there is a real distance between the two.

The most obvious difference has already been stated: teachers get paid, and parents do not. This is so obvious—why mention it? It is important because teachers can, and do, stop teaching. They go home at night, and have another life of their own without students. Parents never stop. They are parents 24/7 and are holistic in their perspective. They have these children for life, all of life with all of its complexity and uncertainty. Therefore, they tend to be conservative and comfortable with what they know, that is, their own childhood experience. After all, they turned out all right, didn't they?

Teachers are more limited than parents. They see the students for a short time, whether that be hours, days, or years. During that time, they are expected to focus on a limited aspect of the student's development. During this period of time, teachers want to be effective and make a real difference in their students' lives. They may be willing to experiment with new ways of accomplishing this. However, if they are not wonderfully successful or if the experiment does not work as well as hoped, teachers can turn away and try something different next time.

Additionally, teachers are generally not as personally invested in the success of a particular student as parents are. For many parents, the success or failure of the student is an issue with implications about them personally. As a result, parents tend to have stronger reactions about what their child does or does not do. Parents may vacillate between pride and panic. Teachers, at least experienced ones, have seen all of this before, and while they may be proud, very proud, of their students, they tend not to panic when things go awry. Parents may see this calmness as an indication of callousness at best and disdain at worst. This perception can poison parent-teacher interactions to the point of open antagonism.

There are some parents with whom the teacher has virtually no interaction. Teachers often make the assumption that these are part-time, or uncaring, parents uninterested in the fate of their children. There may indeed be some parents like that, but they are very rare. The difference here is not in caring or interest, but in time and energy. Teachers have the time and interest to spend about a third of their life with students. The majority of parents have to spend about a third of their lives working in jobs that are physically demanding, stressful, and often not much fun. It is not surprising that they fail to be involved in their child's education. It is enough that the child is safe, entertained, and, perhaps, learning the three R's.

Teachers might be defined as professional adults. This is very different, and more limited, than any reasonable definition of "parent," but an alliance between parents and teachers can work miracles for the child, and must be fervently cultivated.

WHO TEACHES: AN EXAMPLE

Some people know, almost from the day they are born, they will be a teacher. But most of us are accidental teachers; we teach because it happened to work out that way. In my case, I had graduated from college, and was looking for my first serious job. To put it bluntly, I did not set the world aflame as a college kid. It was the 1960s, and there were more interesting things happening in the street than in the classroom. So I received a very liberal education; it just did not show up on the transcript.

There were two possible jobs. The first was selling corporate jets to corporate America. The territory was about half the country, the perquisites were wonderful, and the salary was huge. The second job was to teach in an all-boy boarding school with dorm duty every other night and weekend for a truly tiny salary plus room and board.

It was no contest. On August 15, I signed my contract to start after Labor Day.

I had not planned on teaching, and certainly had done nothing to prepare myself for teaching. However, in retrospect, it seems that the choice was a foregone conclusion. First, there were those wonderful vacations; imagine having the whole summer to roll around doing nothing but having fun. Second, I did not see myself as a salesman. And third, I had been taught by some teachers I admired and even loved.

Many teachers have gone straight from college to teaching because they did not want to give up their summer breaks. The more self-reflective might say that they really did not want to do anything for a solid twelve months, and the summer would allow them a change of pace or focus. The more hedonistic just want ten weeks with nothing scheduled. There is that old cliché that if it looks too good to be true, it probably is too good to be true. Yes, the summer is a change, but it is not free. It is work to make more money or to get more education and training. Teachers may have the time, but rarely have the funds to just roll around enjoying themselves. If teachers want to do more than sit in the backyard dreaming of far-off places, they have to work.

What I did not know about sales would have filled a good-size bookshelf. I did not know any salesmen, and the only model I had was the *Music Man*. Of course, in the end, he was redeemed. But in the 1960s, people my age saw themselves as the redeemers, not the redeemed. I find it ironic now that teaching is mostly a sales job. I spend my day selling myself and my subject to the students, selling the students to themselves, selling students to colleges, sometimes selling students to their parents, and occasionally selling an idea for change to my fellow teachers. At its core, good teaching is all about good sales.

I have asked many teachers about their teachers. In every case, they can name at least one important teacher in their lives. Great teaching produces a pool of potential teachers; the teaching profession recruits its members young. And because beginning teachers tend to model themselves after those important teachers, it is a profession that is literally handed down from generation to generation. I was lucky: I had four extraordinary teachers. Did I have any choice but to teach?

WHO TEACHES: WHO THEY ARE

If good teaching creates a pool of potential teaching candidates, there must be a huge number of people who might be teachers and are not. So who are those who become teachers?

Historically many of them are women; especially in the elementary schools. This may be a last vestige of traditional gender roles. Anecdotally, it seems more men are moving into elementary schools than ever before. In high schools, the division is more equal except in the sciences and technology departments, where men remain predominant. But overall, there are still more women than men teaching in the K–12 schools.

Public school teachers have more often graduated from public universities and independent schoolteachers more often from private universities. As a group, teachers do not come from the top 10 percent of their graduating class. Students with the highest grades and test scores were the least likely among their peers to enroll in education classes or teacher training programs.[1]

Be that as it may, teachers are very likely to continue to graduate school. Unlike other professions that use graduate degrees as gatekeepers, teachers do not absolutely need a master's to start teaching. Certainly, they will get paid more if they have a master's, or two. However, they have to get the degree on their own time, at night or during the summer. And frequently, they pay the tuition themselves. The payback rate, in increased salary, is not fast, and it is even slower for work beyond the master's degree. A possible explanation for this behavior is that teachers value education in and of itself.

In addition, those who become teachers tend to have socially liberal values but, equally, tend to be conservative in their personal spheres. The philosophy of every school speaks of creating upstanding citizens supporting the American core values. I have never met a teacher who does not support and try to teach those values. It is because they see, on a daily basis, how those values are subverted by economics, location, race, and community that they tend to vote liberal. Obviously not every teacher is a social liberal. But if all the teachers were on a ship, and the political liberals went left with the conservatives going right, the ship would capsize in a heartbeat.

What separates the few from the many in the pool of potential teachers is not just valuing education, nor their GPAs, nor their amalgam of liberal conservatism. Those may be necessary but not sufficient explanations. What really sets teachers apart are two traits. The first is that teachers are idealists. To a person, they believe the world can be a better place and they, all by themselves, can make a difference, and, perhaps, a big difference. There is no single vision of a world made new. Teachers have their own visions, and every day, when they walk into class, they are working towards making those visions real.

The second trait that really sets teachers off from the mainstream is a willingness to spend the majority of their professional lives in the presence of children or teenagers. This single fact sets teachers

off from almost every other professional. I will not try to explain it;
it is just a true statement. But in most cases, it seems to be a benign
abnormality that frequently maintains a youthfulness and vigor on
the part of those who enjoy it.

WHO TEACHES: RISK TAKERS

I have been told off and on over the last thirty years, that teachers
tend not to be big risk takers. Most often this kind of comment
comes from my more entrepreneurial acquaintances who feel they
have risked much to gain success, and wear that risk-taking as a
badge of honor.

Often, with this comment comes a second thought, which is that
teachers, lacking the risk-taking, do not deserve to be paid more than
they already are. In short, teachers are too comfortable with the status quo; they have a sinecure as long as they do not rock the boat.
They get up in the morning and do not put on a power tie, nor do
they dress for success, nor do they do power lunches or power naps.
They hardly ever read books about management by the minute. On
the other hand, they will dress in something comfortable and worn,
unless it's September or December. They will carry a sack lunch, and
hope they can last until dismissal. Teachers are not the ones manning
the barricades in the forefront of social or commercial change.

None of this is surprising given that most teachers are personal
conservatives. While many are charismatic, they are not high-profile
personalities. Most have very little desire to be in the limelight and
are kind of embarrassed if they find themselves there.

If teaching is mostly about sales, teachers have to do a high-stakes
sales job every day, especially at the start of a year, or new class.
However, unlike most salespeople, teachers have to face their clients
for up to 180 days. If they oversell, undersell, or fail to sell at all,
they are faced with twenty to thirty clients who can make their lives
miserable, if not a living hell. This fact makes walking into the classroom for the first time a very high-risk situation. Sure, it gets easier

after a few years, but many experienced teachers get wound up tight every September because "this is the year they will hate me."

During the year, the teacher faces ongoing risks, especially in high school, where teenagers do not grant respect and authority easily. Each day is different. Almost anything from a rainy day to a lost football game can change the tenor of the class, and the teacher can become the focus for all that angst. You have to read the class the moment they come through the door or lose them. If you lose them, life is not a bed of roses.

To respond to these vagaries, teachers have to be open, somewhat trusting, ready to listen, and willing to reach out to the student. This makes the teacher vulnerable. Action from a position of vulnerability is the definition of taking a risk. No, it is not the risk of a police officer or a soldier, most of the time. But it is a personal risk with very personal consequences. George Martin in his biography of Verdi makes the comment, "Nothing is more agitating, even physically painful to a teacher, than to realize that, somehow, he is failing to hold the full attention of his best and favorite student. It is like a personal repudiation."[2] Are teachers any more risk-aversive than anybody else? No, they are not.

WHO TEACHES: GAYS, LESBIANS, AND HETEROSEXUALS

Can a gay or lesbian be a successful teacher? The short answer to this question is, maybe. There are certainly schools and communities where it would not work. On the other hand, most schools and most communities have adopted a benign version of the "don't ask, don't tell" policy.

I have been at several schools where open gays and lesbians were accepted and respected members of the faculty and administration. And I have been at a school where a lesbian was terminated at year's end. However, there were some ambiguities in this case. Was she let go because she was a lesbian, or was she let go because she announced, with no warning to the administration, to a school-wide assembly that she was a lesbian?

A more general question, and the one that must be answered, is what is the role of sexuality in teaching? Every teacher has a sexual identity and history, be it male, female, gay, lesbian, or even, young or old. The myth is that teachers leave all that behind, and become asexual, androgynous beings when they teach. Of course, like many myths, this one is patently untrue. So the urgent question is, how is it dealt with?

The question is most urgent for teachers fresh out of college, especially if teaching in high school. The question is urgent because there is not a great age difference between student and teacher and because, for the first time in most teachers' lives, they have real power. The issue is further compounded by the fact that students of virtually any age can develop a crush on a teacher. So how do teachers deal with this?

I have never seen a course in teacher education colleges addressing the issue, and I've never seen a formal discussion of it, except in one school where the head of school simply told all incoming teachers, "Do not hit on the students." With that one exception, the sexual identity of teachers has been generally ignored, at least at the formal level.

On the informal level, the issue is dealt with in a number of ways, conscious and unconscious. First, new teachers are recruited to the profession by teachers they know, respect, and are comfortable with. Very few students are comfortable with teachers who wear their sexuality on their sleeve. Therefore, since most new teachers model themselves after their favorite teachers, the issue is taken care of almost automatically.

Secondly, most schools have formal or informal dress codes for the faculty. These codes create a social distance between the students and the faculty. I have been at schools where most faculty males below a certain age wore beards and the women wore long skirts; virtually none of the students did either. At most schools, a tie worn on a high school campus immediately sends a strong message of social distance.

Thirdly, while I have never heard the issue discussed openly at any faculty meeting, teachers know that this issue is dynamite, and they control it themselves using all kinds of social pressure including humor, comments, rumors, and, occasionally, outright ostracism and complaints to the administration.

In other words, it is no accident that teachers will never be on the cover of any style magazine unless it is called *The Frumpy Quarterly*.

WHY NOT TO TEACH: SALARY

Why does anybody decide to go into teaching? If you ask teachers this question, you get an astounding range of answers, many of them incoherent and, probably, not rational. After all, the free market economists will tell you that rational people will maximize their return on effort. If this is true, teachers are not rational. In the year 2002, the average beginning salary for a new B.A. was about $40,000, but the average new teacher earned about $31,000, a difference of over 22 percent. In the same year, the average, midlevel accountant earned about $54,000, the average computer analyst $74,000, and the average engineer $76,000, while the average teacher earned about $44,000.[3] So, the decision to teach is not about money.

Statistics, especially averages, are slippery things, and it is hard to know exactly what these numbers mean. However, it is as clear as a bell that teachers do not get paid as other professions do. There may be many reasons for this disparity. First, teaching has historically been the work of women, and a women's profession is not going to be paid as well as a man's. Second, education has been predominantly a public sector institution and the public sector is simply not paid as well as the private. Third, since most Americans have been through high school, they consider themselves somewhat expert, and they are not sure there is very much to teaching; why pay a lot for something anybody can do? And finally, teachers work only about 190 days a year compared to 240 or so days that other professionals work.

Whatever the reasons, and several of the reasons cited are myths, there is a significant financial downside to teaching. If teachers live where most of the students are, in any state bordering open water, they are going to struggle to buy a condo, much less a house. Often the students will drive nicer, newer cars than they do. And vacations to the Bahamas or the ski resorts are probably going to be rare.

In addition, extra retirement savings are probably difficult, if not out of the question. It is true that some school systems and several states have excellent retirement systems for teachers. But for the most part, the low salaries translate to low social security benefits and low retirements.

For these reasons, teachers often have a second job. A favorite is working in the big bookstore chains. And for these reasons, married teachers have been dual-income families far longer than has been fashionable, and, maybe for these reasons, more women teach than men. A teacher's income may be fine if it is the second income, but it's a fairly marginal, middle-class primary income.

If the decision to teach is not about money, the decision not to teach often is about money. Teachers leave the profession in droves within the first five years of their careers. To some extent this is understandable; they go back to school, they get married, they become lawyers. What is more frightening is that many teachers at all stages of their careers walk away and never come back. Why? Most often, it is simply the salary. Teachers with five years experience are just hitting their stride. They know how the school works, and they have some idea of how to run their classroom. If history is any guide, the salary they earn as a five-year veteran will be about what they earn as a twenty-five year veteran, in inflation-adjusted dollars. As the numbers in the first paragraph show, the longer you teach, the farther behind you fall.

WHY NOT TO TEACH: STATUS

Salary is the weakest reason to teach and, probably, the greatest reason not to teach for most teachers. But there are other reasons not to teach. Primary among these is the status of teachers, with parents, students, and the public at large. When I was a second-year teacher, I needed to buy tires for my car. In the course of a discussion with the tire salesman, he asked what I did, and I allowed as how I was a high school science teacher. His response was, "Well, that doesn't put you very high on the intellectual totem pole." The fact that I can quote him indicates the blow I felt to my pride. Sure, I got over it; because I was spending time on race courses, I knew more about tires than he did, but I sometimes wonder about his automatic assumption that teachers were just not very intellectual.

Status is at the crux of the many issues facing teachers. First, when state budgets get cut, do firemen's salaries get cut? No. Do police salaries get cut? No. And nobody wants them cut. Do teacher salaries get cut? Inevitably, and generally first. The actual salaries may not get cut, but the jobs get expanded by more classes, or more students per class, or fewer supplies, and more out-of-pocket expenses for teachers. Even when state law requires specific annual salary increases, those increases simply may not be funded. To do so would require tax adjustments either in kind or amount, and the general public, especially those holding real estate, will not support such adjustments.

Secondly, good teaching looks effortless when seen from the student's perspective. Almost all adults remember what they think they saw while sitting in class; they ignore the fact that they saw with the eyes of a child. Therefore, the general feeling is that teaching is easy. How hard can it be to have students learn the multiplication tables or the parts of a cell?

The low status of teachers is confirmed by the politicians. Whenever and however the shortcomings of schools are the subject of political dialogue, the culprits are always the teachers and/or the teachers' unions. There is rarely any discussion of the role of parents, school boards, budgets, aging and crowded structures, or even students. The message is always that the problem is the teacher.

However, it must be said that no matter what the status of the profession is, individual master teachers may be, and often are, lionized by the community they serve. The movie *Mr. Holland's Opus* is not all that far-fetched. In addition, many, many teachers have gotten a great deal of support from their communities including breaks on mortgage rates, service for their cars, and in one case in particular, absolutely free medical care for the birth of their child. It happens, especially in smaller communities, but it happens to individuals, not the profession, and it happens for those individuals who have made an unusual commitment to the community and to teaching.

WHY TEACH: LOVERS AND HEIRS

So why teach? There may be no good reasons to teach unless you are a dreamer in love. Really good teachers are always in love. It really does not matter what they love. They may love their subject. They may love teaching, or they may love being around their students. Whatever it is, it's that love that gets them up in the morning. It's that love that gives them a level of excitement that lasts all day and leaves them drained in the evening. If that love dies, what is left is ugly, often bitter, somewhat cynical, and always damaging to students.

The master teachers I have known and watched loved all three: their subject, the act of teaching, and their students. When asked why they taught, many of these teachers answered with the old clichés, "I do not teach science, history, English, etc., I teach students. Yes, I love my subject, but it is only the vehicle for change and growth in my kids. If I teach it right, I can see it happen in front of my eyes." These may be clichés, but they are clichés precisely because they are true.

Some folks spend their lives perfecting, building, and selling gizmos. Some folks, like stockbrokers, spend their lives selling and, maybe, delivering dreams. And some folks spend their lives making everything else work. Any one of these, and many more, may be wonderful ways to pass a lifetime, but none of them can hold a candle to helping to build a really fine human being. Everybody has moments of success, but teachers see it every time the kids' eyes light up when they see and understand something never seen and never understood before. Does it happen every day? No, but it happens often enough to keep the teacher coming back for more, or the teacher leaves, and does something else for a lifetime.

Every now and then on a slow news day, the local paper runs a story about someone with lots of children, grandchildren, and great-grandchildren. It's all about heirs. How many heirs does a teacher have? Certainly when I was raising my child, I passed on to her many of the ideas and attitudes that I had learned from my teachers. Equally certain is the fact that she added to them and changed them when she made them her own, but still, my teachers are there in her life. It's just like DNA; modified and diluted but passed on from generation to generation. By the time he retires, every good teacher has hundreds of heirs.

Perhaps this is the best reason to teach. Teachers dream a better world and have a capacity to achieve that dream not for just one generation but certainly two and possibly three generations. There are others who can make that claim. Certainly parents do, but parents are limited by biology. Teachers are not. Scientists can make the claim, but only a few succeed. Virtually any teacher, even those forgotten or those you wish you could forget, can make the claim and have it be true.

WHY TEACH: WHO'S IN CHARGE?

There is another reason to teach. Several years ago, I read some research that said teachers and orchestra conductors had the longest life spans of any professions.[4] This is not a suggestion that you should teach in order to eke out a year or two of extra existence. The real question is why should teachers live long? The suggested answer was that teachers and conductors both had control over precisely how and what they do. That degree of control means that they suffer less stress than others.

Once the door closes and class begins, the teachers are on their own. Schools generate a great many rules, procedures, and limits on what teachers do in the classroom. However, a teacher faced with twenty or more students is thrust into a situation that is so highly variable that no set of rules, procedures, or limits can possibly address the details of what happens next.

Success as a teacher is determined by hundreds of decisions made on the fly, based on intuition, during every class period. Each of those decisions is made without anybody looking over your shoulder, second-guessing your actions. You are in control of your own destiny as a teacher. Nobody gets it right all of the time. If you blow it too many times, you will be mediocre at best. If you get it right more often than not, you will be a good teacher. If you get it right most of the time, you are a master teacher. After getting it right for a while, students will forgive and protect a teacher from all but the most egregious errors.

Even in large schools where several teachers are teaching the same subject, the teachers are not in lockstep. Visit the classrooms of two teachers teaching the same material and the classrooms will be different. They will be different in tone, in content and approach.

It is no accident that teachers and conductors are blessed with longevity. Both are given a broad mandate to develop and synthesize beauty out of the actions of others, according to a score open to interpretation, artistry, and play. Just as every conductor imprints a performance, every aspect of the classroom is permeated by the teacher's personality. The teacher, *qua* artist, constructs, sculpts, and colors every part and function of the classroom. The conductor does not play the music, and the teacher cannot define the classroom. There are other independent agents, musicians or students, working in the same space, but, to a greater degree than most other professionals, conductors and teachers shape their immediate work environment and, more important, the immediate outcomes of their efforts.

Done well, teaching is the act of creating a beautiful performance including multiple solos along with ensembles in multiple voices and timbres. There can be no greater fulfillment, satisfaction, or sense of well-being than that generated by such a performance. There is no question; good teaching is worth living for.

MASTER TEACHER TRAITS

What do teachers have to know when they walk into the classroom? There is no question that teachers have to know whereof they teach. There is no question that a teacher only a chapter ahead of the students lacks the depth required to make the classroom a fascinating place; if only because he or she cannot make the connections between the classroom material and the rest of the students' lives.

One of the struggles of young teachers is always that they do not, and cannot, know their subject well enough to generate the richness of connections found in the master teacher's class, where student questions always lead to where the teacher wants to go. However, that richness may come over time. It is a cliché that you cannot really know a subject until you have taught it for a while.

An in-depth understanding of the subject is a necessary prerequisite to successful teaching, but it is not sufficient. I once taught at a school where the majority of teachers had Ph.D.'s. The school did not have a surfeit of master teachers. There was no visible correlation between having a Ph.D. and excellence in the classroom. Successful teachers also have a life story that resonates with the students. To the extent that students see teachers as automatons, wheeled into closets at the closing bell, and plugged in until the next morning, both teachers and subjects lack credibility. To the extent that teachers bring a multidimensionality into the classroom based on real-world experience admired by students, both the teacher and the subject have credibility. It is not a requirement that the story be directly connected to the subject. A history teacher does not have to live history. But he has to live. And he has to live outside of the classroom, and he has to bring his life into the classroom.

In addition to competence and life experience, master teachers have compassion, where compassion means the ability to meet the students where they are. To meet students where they are means not only to understand their worldview of the moment, but to be able to translate the subject into analogies and metaphors that make sense to the student.

Given that you have competence, experience, and compassion, how do you learn to teach? That is a crucial question for which we have not developed very good answers. One answer is to allow people to live for a while, and then certify them as teachers on the basis of their experience. A second answer is to send would-be teachers to school to learn how to teach. The third answer is to throw would-be teachers into the classroom, and see if they survive. Each of these approaches has advantages and disadvantages. Each of these approaches will lead to very different first four or five years for the nascent teacher. But truth be told, after five years, it does not seem to make any difference at all how master teachers learned their trade.

BECOMING A TEACHER: INDEPENDENT SCHOOLS

New teachers in private, independent schools endure a baptism of fire. Many, probably most, independent schools have the attitude that they hire good, bright people, and the schools throw them into the classroom to sink or swim. If the school is progressive, it may set up a semi-formal mentoring system where an experienced teacher leads the tyro through the major mine fields of report cards, parents' night, and other arcane aspects of how the school works.

Usually the mentor is a full-time teacher, carrying a full workload, and does not have a great deal of time to give the novice. Nor does the mentor define himself as a practitioner of adult education. Adult education is very different in the approach taken, and in the techniques used. In addition, because of schedule conflicts, the mentor generally cannot spend a great deal of time watching the novice actually teach.

Therefore, the mentor is most often reduced to monitoring the tyro's morale, and putting out fires after they have gotten started well enough to seriously burn the novice. Does this approach work? Yes and no. It is very expensive in terms of wasted talent and wasted opportunity. A high percentage of the good, bright people that independent schools hire leave the profession within one, two, or three years. Often they leave in tears swearing never to return. Often the given reasons are graduate school, or just plain burnout. But for young, energetic, excited teachers, burnout should be rare, especially in the suburban independent school. That it is a common reason for leaving condemns the approach. Graduate school may be a legitimate reason for leaving teaching but may not be a legitimate reason to stay away. The fact that few new teachers return with an advanced degree condemns the approach.

The only reason that this approach works at all is because independent schools are full of the best teachers-of-teachers that have ever existed, the students. When a new teacher enters the class for the first time, the students start working to make the novice meet their expectations. The methods include off-the-cuff jokes and questions, comments, smiles, resistance, and sometimes, rejection.

More often than not it is the students who explain the school to the new teacher. The administration will tell the teacher how the school should work, and the students will tell the teacher how it actually works. To be sure, the students have a particular viewpoint, but they have a vested interest in making the class work. For better or worse, most students, most of the time in most independent schools, have personal, parental, and social pressures to succeed. It is to their advantage to have happy, effective teachers, and they will work to create them.

The relationship between the teacher and the guides is tenuous, more like a spider web than a cargo net, and distant. The questions and answers are rarely explicit. The students generally will not intentionally mislead the teacher, but this system will fail if the teacher does not have the competence, experience, or compassion to connect with the students. It is the kiss of death for a new teacher not to recognize that the students are his allies, but it is equally disastrous to throw oneself on their mercy. Either leads to a one or two year career path ending in tears.

BECOMING A TEACHER: THE UNIVERSITY

The most common way of learning something about teaching is to attend undergraduate and/or graduate education courses. Education courses are held in disdain at many universities. They are considered to be the university's corporate pro-bono work. In part, this is the result of the fact that teachers have a low professional status and in part because the material is less theoretical and more applied than most courses. More important is the failure to recognize that schools and schooling are inherently far more complex systems than anything most departments deal with, and there are, therefore, few agreed upon "right" answers. One can mock courses about how to put together bulletin boards, but then, maybe, one should mock schools of art. One can mock courses on group dynamics and communication, but recognize that much of a business school curriculum is about the same material.

One valuable group of courses about the social foundations of education includes psychology, sociology, history, and anthropology as they apply to education and schools. Without these courses, or their equivalents, the teacher would not be exposed to the major learning theories of behaviorism, cognitivism, or constructivism. Without this background, the phrase, "different strokes for different folks" will not call to mind Bloom's taxonomy of learning or Gardner's various types of intelligences. Nor will the statement that "single-sex boarding schools with their academic gothic architecture are the last sanctioned trace of medievalism in the U.S." make any sense at all. In short, absent these courses, or their equivalent, teachers have little context in which to practice their craft, and the best of them will have to reinvent the wheel.

More important, schools of education have a mentoring system that actually works. It is called student teaching. Student teaching works because individuals voluntarily commit to make it work both at the university level and the classroom level. The student teacher is watched, critiqued, monitored, and supported constantly by at least two other adults. Virtually every action, every breath the student teacher takes is analyzed, and commented on. In fact this is often so true that more than a few potential teachers have dropped out at this stage of their training because of the stress of always being watched.

Most student teaching experiences last a trimester or semester. The student always says that a semester is plenty long enough, and experienced teachers say that maybe it is not quite long enough. In any case, the advantages of student teaching are huge when compared to the alternative of not student teaching. The student teaching experience is often the first time that the student teacher gets to see teaching from the adult side of the big desk. All their previous experience of teaching has been as a student. From the student's perspective, some huge percentage of teaching is invisible. Schools of education may not be the leading edge of education, but more than anything else, they are the most efficient way for the would-be teacher to develop competence and compassion.

BECOMING A TEACHER: MID-CAREER CHANGE

The least common and most recent development in teacher training is to recruit new teachers from the ranks of mid-career adults. The goal here is to recruit teachers who are five or more years beyond college. They have been doing something else with their lives, often military careers, and for one reason or another decide they want to be teachers. People at this stage generally cannot afford to go back to school; after all they most likely have children themselves, have mortgages, and almost certainly have credit cards. But they also have a maturity and wealth of experience to bring to the classroom that most new teachers do not. Further, many of these folks bring with them an in-depth understanding of technical areas of math, science, and technology that is hard to beat. Therefore, these candidates are too valuable a resource to ignore.

In response, a majority of states have put together programs to move these people into the classroom in a streamlined fashion with either no or minimal interruption of cash flow. Of course, the cash may not be as good as it was before they made the decision to teach, but at least it is there.

If the first prerequisite to being a master teacher is competence, the advantage of this kind of program is that the would-be teacher does not have to spend time on developing competence. Almost all the people who enter such a program expect to teach something they have both academic and practical experience with.

If the second prerequisite is life experience that can be brought into the classroom, these candidates, especially the "troops to teachers" folks, often have that in spades. In addition, many of these candidates have decades of life experience. I have taught with many who came to teaching after twenty or thirty years in other careers. The character they brought to their classes was extraordinary. Their classes were always relevant to their students.

The third prerequisite is compassion; being able to meet the student where he is at the moment. Compassion is a tough thing to teach. But these programs have several characteristics that make them successful doing so. First, they tend to be small and cohort-based. They generally start during the summer and last through a school year. Although the candidates know when they start where they are going and what they will be doing, during the summer the cohort forms strong ties based on shared uncertainties about just what they are getting into. During the year, while teaching full-time, they meet regularly for course work and mutual support. In addition, they have mentors committed to seeing their program work. In short, these new teachers get far more structural and personal support during that traumatic first year than any other kind of program affords.

Further, many of these people have been in positions of power and leadership before. They know the basics of management in a way that no other group of new teachers does.

The net result is that these programs tend to be very successful both in getting potential master teachers into the profession and in keeping them in the profession. The retention rate for these teachers tends to be much higher than those from other kinds of recruitment and training programs. The only drawback is that many districts have contracts that limit where new teachers can enter the pay scale. That means that a person with twenty years of experience in the sciences or math may only get the salary of a teacher with four or five years of experience. That's too bad.

NOTES

1. "Teaching at Risk: A Call to Action," The Teaching Commission, 2004. Retrieved January 12, 2008, from http://ftp.ets.org/pub/corp/ttcreport .pdf, p.17.

2. G. W. Martin, *Verdi* (New York: Limelight editions, 1992).

3. H. F. Nelson and R. Drown, "Survey and Analysis of Teacher Salary Trends 2002," American Federation of Teachers, 2003. Retrieved December 15, 2007, from http://www.aft.org/salary/2002/download/SalarySurvey02 .pdf.

4. D. G. Myers, *The Pursuit of Happiness: Who Is Happy—and Why* (New York: William Morrow and Company, 1992).

CHAPTER 2

What to Teach

WHAT TO TEACH: HISTORICITY, PART 1

So you have a license, or not, to teach. As you walk into class on the first day, it is to be devoutly hoped that somewhere previous to that day, you have answered the question, "What are my goals as a teacher?" The answers to this question cannot be simply to keep good order and discipline, or to teach art, history, or science. These goals may be sufficient for a month or two but they are too mono-chromatic to support a career.

The Internet will give you tens of thousands of hits about the goals of education. Some sites are written from the social perspective of producing effective, entrepreneurial, technically astute workers and citizens. Some sites are written from the student perspective of self-actualization, social mobility, and happiness.

It is possible to bring these views together using historicity.[1] His-toricity is the ability of a society or an individual to intervene in their own existence to change or re-invent themselves. There are three necessary, mutually causal components of historicity: the knowledge and skills to intervene, the fiscal or social capital to underwrite the intervention, and a worldview to carry out, support, and give mean-ing to the intervention.

From a national perspective, the goal of education is to make sure that every student has, at least, the minimum knowledge and skills to intervene in his or her own life, that is, get a job, read directions, fill out tax forms, and so on. Society would also very much appreci-ate teachers inculcating the student with a worldview that made get-ting a job and filling out taxes a meaningful intervention in their own lives. And society has invested a degree of fiscal and social capital in making this happen.

The student's perspective on the goal of education is very similar to the national goals. The student wants to have the knowledge and skills to get a high-paying job, to read the sales contract for a new car, and to pay the lowest possible taxes. And the student expects to get happiness out of these activities and has invested social and fiscal capital in the form of lost opportunity costs.

Therefore there is little or no difference, overall, between the national and individual goals of education in this country. But the devil is in the details. As this is being written, there are several deep and substantive social schisms developing in all three of historicity's components. When President Kennedy proposed going to the moon, he was proposing a massive intervention in our society. First and foremost it had meaning; it was the new frontier. Second, we had the manpower or social capital to invest, and Kennedy had the personal social capital to serve as seed money. In addition, we had the fiscal capital to make it happen. And finally, as a society we had or could develop the technical knowledge to make it happen.

When President Bush proposed going to Mars, he also was proposing a massive intervention, but this time the proposal sank like a stone. Not only did he not have sufficient personal social capital, but the nation did not have the fiscal or social capital to support the effort. The technical knowledge and skills existed or could be developed, but the national worldview had fractured, and did not give meaning to the effort; the will was not there.

WHAT TO TEACH: HISTORICITY, PART 2

If the goal of teaching is to increase the student's historicity, the master teacher cannot focus solely, or even primarily, on the transmission of information. Rather, the teacher must have three foci: the transmission of knowledge and skills, the accrual of social capital, and the development of a worldview that gives meaning to the students' interventions in their own and others' lives.

The formal job description for any teaching position focuses primarily on the transmission of knowledge and skills. I am hired to be a history, Spanish, or art teacher, and that is what I expect to do. Imagine my surprise if hired to teach science, I discover in August that I am assigned an art class and a French class starting in September. I will not last long, not just because both the students and I am frustrated, but because I am not transmitting the correct sorts of knowledge and skills.

However, the transmission of knowledge and skills is only one-third, and probably the easiest and most straightforward third, of any effort to increase historicity. It is the other two-thirds, increasing the student's social capital and the development of meaning, that count the most towards creating successful, happy individuals able to intervene in their own, and others', lives.

Consider for the moment the perfect squirrel. The perfect squirrel lives in a tree, builds a nest, collects nuts both for today and the future, and mates to produce a lot of little squirrels. Squirrels that do all this successfully are indeed perfect. To the extent that they can stay safe in the tree, collect more and more nuts, and produce more and more offspring, they are more and more perfect. These may be admirable activities, but all this is about the squirrels themselves and nothing else.

The existentialists such as Camus[2] argue that that there is essentially no difference between the squirrel and a person except that the person can become fully human and fully alive by committing to something larger, better, and outside of self. It is not so much what we do that makes us different from the squirrel. It is our commitment to why we do it that may separate us from the squirrel. The individual with no social capital is in desperate straits, and any intervention is about survival, but any individual, even with lots of social capital, who intervenes only for self may be very impressive, but is still no better than a squirrel.

The "why" we commit, and to some extent the "what" we commit to, is the result of character. The structure of our character is based on our ideas about the nature of Self, Others, the Universe, Knowledge, Truth, and Value. Every teacher with a few years of experience can name students who were perfect squirrels and were, not always for the same reasons, nightmares to have in class.

Most teachers have never heard of the concept of historicity as it is used here, but every master teacher intuitively understands that there is more to successful teaching than a single focus on knowledge and skills. In fact, it is probably impossible to teach just knowledge and skills. But to the extent that such becomes the criterion of success, we will tend to produce squirrels.

HISTORICITY: KNOWLEDGE & SKILLS

The first component of historicity is knowledge and skill. Every teacher agrees that students need a certain minimum knowledge to survive, be happy, and be successful, and no teacher willfully denies students that content. But what is that knowledge? Such knowledge certainly includes knowing how to tie your shoes, but does it include knowing what a gerund is, being able to solve differential equations, recognizing Avogadro's number, or understanding Turner's thesis about the impact of the frontier on American culture?

There are individuals for whom each of these is crucially important, but that individuality is precisely the point. A teacher responsible for just twenty students is faced with such a variety of present and future trajectories that it is virtually impossible to discern what each student needs to know. So how do you decide what to teach?

One possible answer is to decide on a list of facts, concepts, and ideas or skills thought to be central to the American culture, and make sure the curriculum contains all those elements.[3] The list is fairly expansive, and is going to consume a lot of time and effort, but might be quite valuable if all the students are all the same. On a lighter note, another list[4] says that everything you need to know can be taught in kindergarten and the next twelve years can be spent on other pursuits. These two lists are very different. The one is onerous but limited, retrogressive, specific and, frankly, tedious to teach, to learn, or to be held accountable to. The second is short but inclusive, affirming, and progressive. Which list would you choose?

Unfortunately, you do not have a choice. More and more, schooling is driven by the onerous but limited, retrogressive, specific and tedious lists at the core of all standardized testing. Now, testing certainly serves some purpose. It provides a very limited benchmark as to the quality of teaching that goes on. But this is a very limited benchmark that makes the assumptions that all students are the same, that all subcultures are the same, and that every thing on the test is of equal utility. None of these assumptions can be true.

But there is a much more dangerous aspect to these lists. The contents of the lists are safe. There is nothing dangerous about subject-verb agreements or the quadratic equations. But can you imagine an AP science test asking about stem cell research or an AP history test asking about My Lai? Do you really think anybody would sit still for a multiple choice, SAT question on safe sex? No, the lists of technical knowledge on which these test are built are very, very safe.

At worst, safe means trivial. At best, safe means accepted by virtually everybody. The rate of change in the knowledge available to students is increasing, but much of that new knowledge is not acceptable to virtually everybody. That means that every day there is more and more knowledge that we hope the students somehow pick up in the street.

There are no easy, universal answers here. The teacher has to decide based on experience what students must know in addition to what the test demands. It is clear that the answer does not lie at the extremes. No testing leads to chaos for the students and no self-evaluation for the teacher. To the extent that testing becomes the be-all and end-all, then we are driving down the road into the future navigating by looking in the rearview mirror at obstacles we have safely passed.

HISTORICITY: THE CRUCIAL SKILLS

Limiting the body of knowledge to what is on the list—to English grammar, quadratic equations, and the like—ignores a crucial body of skills. The knowledge on the list is the students' cultural inheritance. It more or less comes in a box to be stored away or used. But in either case, it is passive the way luggage is passive.

The missing skills are the abilities to make this inheritance the student's own. This is the difference between memorizing and understanding, between having and using. What you remember from school probably differs from what I remember. Why? While we started with much the same luggage, we have been on different trips, and used our luggage differently. What you have used is yours. You made it yours, and you built on it. You do not have to think about it; it is part of the warp and woof of your personality. No teacher can predict with certainty what part of what they teach will be incorporated into students' lives. The best that teachers can do is to provide the skills to make one's education one's own. These skills are difficult to teach, but easy to learn. They can be learned whenever students become responsible for their education.

It can be as simple as asking questions. In most classes, the teacher asks most of the questions. The whole tenor of the class changes if the students ask most of the questions. Good student questions galvanize the class; the students think that the teacher is off the lesson plan, and they pay attention and think about the next question in order to use up the rest of the period. More important, the students become actively involved with the material, and are not just passively receiving bits and pieces to put in their box. The good teacher needs student questions the way a thirsty person needs water. And no matter where the question leads, the master teacher can bring it back to where the students have to go.

On a more formal level, inquiry learning and expeditionary learning[5] accomplish the goal of encouraging students to be active, involved, and in control of their own education. These approaches have three elements in common. The first is that they consume time voraciously. Any combination of expeditionary learning, inquiry-based learning, and question-based learning is going to be less direct, more multifaceted, and less comprehensive than the more teacher-directed approaches.

Second, these approaches incorporate a culture of performance[6] where students must use what they have learned today and yesterday, and possibly in another contexts, to demonstrate to their peers, their teacher, or other audience what they know and understand. Any such demonstration is qualitatively different from answering a test question because it actively integrates some part of the students' knowledge base, and by doing so, they make it their own.

The third element is that asking good questions and applying the answers in one's life are skills that can be learned using parts of those limited, retrogressive, specific and tedious to teach, to learn, or to be held accountable to, lists. But those skills are not tested, and because of time lost, the student will not and cannot know the entire list. That fact will be reflected in student performances on the standardized tests.

Again, there are no easy answers here, we can teach more and use a lot less or we can teach less and use a lot more. Teacher survival calls for the former; student survival calls for the latter.

HISTORICITY: THE POLITICS OF TEACHING

There is one last point to be made about the role of knowledge and skills in the creation of historicity. Knowledge and the access to knowledge have always been politicized. One only has to look at the history of race, gender, and class in this country to understand that fact. Historically, in almost every case, the effort has been to limit the access. More recently, there have been sporadic efforts to increase access. The federal and some state governments have implemented laws and regulations in support of Head Start, Title IX, and affirmative action in an effort to increase student access to knowledge and skills.

Recent, ongoing efforts to deny access include the banning of *Huckleberry Finn* from school and public libraries, the efforts to dilute or prevent the teaching of evolution, or the focus on abstinence in sex education classes. The difference between these efforts and their historic precedents are that these efforts are not primarily aimed at denying access to one race, gender, or class. They are aimed at the whole of society. Further, although they often take the form of laws and regulations, they do not originate within the governing elite to limit the peasants. Rather they originate with subcultures and groups of non-elite, just-plain-folks. Perhaps the most important story of the last twenty years is the story about the battles, federal, state, and local, over who controls the communal knowledge base.

Teachers are political animals. The decisions they make about what knowledge to include in their class is an intensely political act. This fact cannot be avoided because not choosing is an equally political act. College professors have the partial protection of tenure, but most K–12 teachers do not. Safety for many teachers lies in mediocrity, where the definition of mediocrity is what most people do most of the time.

However, master teachers do have a safety net or protection that is not available to mediocre teachers, the trust of their students. Master teachers have compassion; the ability to meet the students where they are. Over time, compassion breeds trust. Over time, trust allows the teacher to shake the students' knowledge base to its foundations, while the students make a conscious effort to protect the teacher. Their conversations with adults other than the teacher will be tailored to avoid getting parents upset or administrators on the prowl.

We have all seen new teachers, inexperienced or just new to the class, try to radically alter the contents of a course. At best, the teacher is viewed as just weird; at worst, the teacher goes down in flames. In every case, the teacher moved too fast. Trust grows organically from the students' previous experiences, the teacher's compassion, and the sociocultural context. It cannot be mandated. It cannot be hurried. The form it takes cannot be predicted. It is fragile but can be self-healing. Once in place, it is likely to be more effective protection than tenure.

If teaching is an intervention to increase the historicity of students, trust is the primary social capital that master teachers have to spend. It underwrites the changes in their own historicity, and it underwrites their interventions in the historicity of their students. It cannot be spent before it is earned, and it must not be squandered, but once in place, it allows the teacher to dramatically alter the historicity of their students. Mutual trust can offset the danger inherent in being a master teacher.

HISTORICITY: ACCRUAL OF CAPITAL

What are the social assets available to students? Some students have status, as an athlete or as a brain, or because of the status of their parents or any one of a hundred other reasons. Status is an important social asset but, by itself, it is often insufficient. The student's peers often resist his attempts to intervene in, or change, his own life. His peers expect him to be today who he was yesterday. If he is not, the question is, "What's wrong with you?" and it will cost him capital, in the form of status and respect, to stay "wrong" until, over time, he becomes "right" again. This peer resistance to change affects adults also, but the flu spreads rapidly in schools precisely because they are close-packed, claustrophobic, and, in a sense, intimate. Under these conditions, peer resistance to student change can be intense, and the cost of change may be more than students, any students, feel they can afford.

While status is usually thought to be earned, it is actually conferred or granted by others, and, therefore, may not be available to every student. What is available to every student is capital generated within the individual in the form of self-confidence and self-awareness. The primary source of such capital is action. Capital is not raised by the student passively watching slides in art history. A tiny bit of capital may be raised if the student has a strong visceral response to what he is seeing, but capital is certainly raised if the student then paints a picture.

The more the student acts, the more internal capital is raised because action is the root source of self-confidence, and/or self-awareness. Action requires risk-taking and independence both of which are sources and outcomes of self-confidence. Action combined with an opportunity for reflection is experience, the source of self-awareness as expressed by "This is who I am and this is what I know, can do, am interested in, and where I want to go." Self-confidence combined with self-awareness is a powerful underwriter of intervention and change.

Teaching is an intervention to increase the historicity of students. Self-awareness and self-confidence are the primary, supporting capital resources master teachers can develop in their students. To do this requires a very fine touch. Self-awareness and self-confidence are mutually causal, and are, especially with students, inherently unstable; they may go up like a rocket and fall like a rock. On any given day, in any given class, some individuals should probably fail, and some absolutely must be successful. And while the identification of those in need of failure or success does not usually change on an hourly basis, it certainly could change on a weekly or, perhaps, daily basis.

The point to be made here is that the passive student does not accrue social or internal capital as rapidly as an active student. Master teachers understand this and provide opportunities for students to act on what they have learned. The good news is that the providing of opportunities for action can be precisely parallel to the providing skills for students to make the knowledge content their own. Having students ask more questions than the teacher, doing inquiry and expeditionary based learning, and, perhaps in this context most important, having a culture of performance in the classroom, will all dramatically increase students' capital and, therefore, their ability to intervene in and change their own lives.

Absent this kind of teaching, the knowledge and skills taught will be inert luggage carried on a voyage but never really unpacked to make a change in the experience or itinerary.

HISTORICITY: WORLDVIEW AND CHARACTER

The third component of students' historicity is their worldview; it is this that gives meaning to life and their interventions to change or create their existence. A worldview is an individual's first principles and ideas about the nature of Self, Others, the Universe, Knowledge, Truth, and Value. These ideas are generally unconscious and unexamined and, sometimes, incoherent or contradictory but they are the basis for an individual's perceiving, thinking, doing, and valuing. For most K–12 students, the source of their worldview is their parents. Other sources include peers, surrogate families such as gangs or cliques, or other significant adults, including teachers.

Most teachers do not set out to teach a worldview. Be that as it may, teachers certainly have the power to alter the students' worldviews, sometimes drastically. Drastic change has become a science and an art in military boot camps, therapeutic high schools, and the twelve-step programs.

The student's worldview places three important constraints on teaching. The first is self-evident and self-explanatory. Because the worldview is so central and pervasive in an individual's existence, the primary rule must be, "Thou shalt do no harm." In this case, harm might be defined as negation or destruction without replacement or substitution; either of which would leave a student adrift.

The second constraint is that these ideas determine what the student learns. They allow the student to assign meaning to knowledge, information, and perceptions. To use an analogy, if perceptions are Christmas ornaments, they make no sense in the box. If they stay in the box, they will not be seen, remembered, or be meaningful. They need to be organized on a tree where the trunk and branches are the student's first principles and ideas. If there is no branch on which to hang the ornament, it is placed back in the box and forgotten. If there is a branch to place it on, it is hung there with its own story to tell both by itself and in relationship to its neighbors in an overall pattern.

Third, the student's worldview structures the attributes of character. A positive and cohesive set of principles and ideas about the nature of Self, Others, the Universe, Knowledge, Truth, and Value will generate integrity tempered by empathy, intelligence tempered by awe, risk-taking tempered by common sense, independence tempered by ethics, leadership tempered by the desire to serve, and most important, self-confidence tempered by self-knowledge.

Without these attributes, academics will not achieve more than mediocrity where the student simply receives wisdom from some external source. In this case, the student is sponge-like, able to absorb and give back, but not necessarily able to add any value. This is the education that, at its best, creates success on standardized tests and, at worst, creates a cult. But it is not an education that supports creativity, inventiveness, or growth.

People may see a great danger in having "just anybody" teaching character; that is understandable as long as character is defined by content. Schools cannot and should not be in the business of teaching the contents of character, certainly not in a society that values individuality, freedom, and diversity. However, schools can legitimately teach the attributes of character.

ATTRIBUTES OF CHARACTER: INTEGRITY

A discussion of character begins with integrity. The students' integrity is based on a set of coherent first principles that give meaning to their perceptions and experiences. Absent a coherent set of first principles, much of what the students learn will not and cannot be used to construct an overarching worldview. Without an overarching worldview, the student will not and cannot have integrity. The signs of integrity are veracity, reliability, and predictability, but integrity is really about the way that the individual plays out the different roles of his existence.

The content of the students' first principles broadly defines their characters. The principles that underlie Ayn Rand's philosophy of Objectivism will produce broadly different sorts of character traits than the principles underlying the Judeo-Christian traditions. To the extent that students consistently use either set of principles to understand and act in varying contexts, they have integrity.

To revisit the analogy of a Christmas tree built of first principles, ornaments in their boxes do not inherently have a pattern. This is the situation when students do not see a connection between their English classes and their French classes or between their math classes and their art classes. The ornaments might be grouped. Over there, we have the history box, here the science box, and somewhere else the math box. There are no connections between the boxes; they exist in isolation. It is the act of placing the ornaments on a branch that connects what has been learned into a coherent pattern.

Imagine for a moment, a tree with only one or, at most, two or three branches. It might be possible to hang a great many ornaments on such a tree. However, the ornaments that could not be hung would be ignored or placed back in a box and forgotten. The resultant pattern could not be as rich, inclusive, or varied as a pattern built on a tree of five, ten, or more branches. We have all known individuals who perceive, understand, and act on the basis on a single idea; some radio talk show hosts are notable for this trait. To put it mildly, their understandings are limited to simplicity, linearity, and reductionism.

The cure for this is empathy, where empathy allows for the possibility that others may, as it were, have differently constructed trees with different ornaments that give equally rich, inclusive, varied, and coherent patterns. Empathy allows the students to examine their own trees in comparison to others to see if they might wish to add or change a branch here and there. Doing so allows for the possibility of change, growth, and maturation of the student's tree with the possibility of adding yet more ornaments.

Integrity and empathy are the beginnings of a foundation of life-long learning. Therefore the goal of the master teacher must be to increase both in students. Radical change can be imposed by the boot-camp approach, but the role of the master teacher is not to directly challenge the first principles of students. To do so runs a risk of doing harm. More often, the master teacher meets the students where they are, establishes a high level of trust, and invests that trust in raising the empathy of the students.

If the teacher has a coherent and explicit worldview of his own, the student will consider all or part of it and may integrate some part into his own worldview. The student may have an epiphany, but usually the integration is not rapid. In fact, it's usually so slow one wonders if anything is happening. To return to the analogy once again, it's a long growing season. What you plant this year may be only a small sprout next year, but may blossom in the years to come.

ATTRIBUTES OF CHARACTER: INTELLIGENCE

A student's intelligence, the second attribute of his character, is a direct outgrowth of his worldview. Intelligence, as the word is used here, is limited to the ability to recognize effective applications of first principles. There are three parts to this recognition. The first, the simplest, is to recognize that one's first principles about others apply to oneself. At almost any time, there are several ongoing cases of high-profile failures to do so; cases where individuals have excoriated others for various behaviors, only to be caught doing the same things themselves. Sometimes, it seems there are some singularly unintelligent folks in radio, television, the pulpit, and Congress.

The second part of intelligence is to recognize when the application of a given principle leads to a case of *reductio ad absurdum*. First principles are, by definition, assumed to be true and valid. However, for any given first principle, you can imagine a situation where following the principle to its logical conclusion will contravene or conflict with one or more other first principles. A classic example is the question for nonviolent conscientious objectors: "Would you use violence to protect your parent, spouse, or child from violence?" A possibly intelligent answer is, "yes"; a "no" taken to extremes would almost certainly contravene one or more basic principles that most of us hold true.

The third part of intelligence is by far the more difficult issue. This intelligence recognizes the uncertainty of first principles in novel situations. In most cases, we analyze novel situations unconsciously by analogy. If the present is similar to the past, we understand and we respond, or not. However, especially when dealing with other people, this approach may be ineffective for one of two reasons. First, because the analogy is unconscious and unexamined, it will reduce the other to a monochrome: for instance, "he does not do homework because he is lazy." Second, the assumption is always that the other person is operating on the same worldview in the same way that I do.

The issues arise from the denial of the inherent complexity of the situation. Intelligence recognizes that human behavior is based on a shifting kaleidoscope of first principles. A few shared first principles can produce complex patterns unlikely to be simultaneously replicated in any two individuals. I hasten to add that there may be an exception to this in mob psychology, but then mobs are precisely unintelligent.

Therefore, intelligence is the antidote to arrogance. Intelligence is about understanding that "sauce for the goose is sauce for the gander," while it holds out the possibility that perhaps the sauce's recipe is not yet perfect nor perfectly understood. Intelligence recognizes the possibility of conflict between first principles and makes sense of uncertainty, shading, complexity, and change. Without intelligence, it would be difficult to grow and maintain integrity.

But intelligence is limited. It has to work within the individual's worldview. There may be novel experiences that simply cannot be given meaning on the basis of first principles. The role of awe gives meaning to those experiences that beggar the intellect. Without awe, how would the individual reach beyond his own boundaries to understand and value that which is forever beyond intellectual reach, like the beauty of a sunset, or the horror of genocide? Can intelligence be taught? That answer is uncertain, but it certainly can be learned. It is equally certain that master teachers can model intelligence in a way that encourages students to develop theirs.

ATTRIBUTES OF CHARACTER: RISK-TAKING

Risk-taking is inherent in exercising historicity. Without risk-taking, students can never explore beyond nor extend received wisdom. Without taking a risk, students are caught in a box not of their own making, but one constructed for them by a teacher; the students can never make the received wisdom their own.

In school, student risk-taking comes in two general forms. The first is to challenge what the students already know, or to extend what they already know to a new context. In short, students question themselves, their principles, and their perceptions. This kind of risk-taking arises, in part, from intelligence and empathy.

The second kind of risk-taking is to challenge or confront what somebody else knows. This type of risk-taking responds to, "I dare you" or "Nobody can do that," or "We think that . . ." or "Everybody knows that . . ."

If there is no cost, then there is no risk. For most students, the potential cost is in terms of the social assets of status, respect, and acceptance. But there is another, more private cost: what does a failed risk, either a risk not taken or one with a negative outcome, do to the student's self-image or confidence? The actual risk-taking is generally a public act, but the decision to risk, or not, is private and based on the student's worldview.

The student has to ask the question of whether the risk and the gain are worth the cost. Common sense provides an answer. But it is a cliché that common sense is not all that common. It is not common because it is an amalgam of intelligence, empathy, and experience. For many people, it makes absolute common sense to play the lottery from time to time. The down side is the loss of some money, but the up side is many, many times the gain. But many lottery players would never step into a casino because the situation does not seem the same. Students constantly do the same kind of risk assessment in class: what is the cost, they wonder, personally and socially, to give the right answer, to give a "funny" answer, or to give no response? Most teachers can name students who never tried; if they never risked and tried, they couldn't fail.

Under these circumstances, risk assessment cannot be taught, but it can be learned. The role of a master teacher is to provide a safe context for taking risks. From the student's perspective this context is one of trust. From the teacher's perspective, the creation of a "safe zone" for risk-taking is also about trust. It is a trust based on the belief that, with very few exceptions, the following statements are true:

- Students are doing the best they know how. This does not necessarily mean they are doing the best math or English or Spanish they know. It means that they are doing the best in life as they know, experience, and feel it. Your interaction with them is only a small part of that complexity.
- Students are not fully developed adults. The statement, "It seemed like a good idea at the time" after a failed risk is probably true. It did. There is increasing evidence that a student's brain is wired differently from an adult's[7] and does not fully develop until the early twenties. Decision-making is different in children and adolescents.
- A mix of success and failure teaches more than constant success. Students have to take risks and fail in order to learn how to do risk assessment. Master teachers, recognizing this, allow the student to risk and fail and then build a soft landing spot so no permanent damage is done. This might be another definition of compassion.

ATTRIBUTES OF CHARACTER: ETHICS

If students take risks, they become independent. Independence is the willingness to spend or discount the social capital required to achieve an end. Independence is the willingness to be different. It allows the student to challenge or confront the group.

However, untrammeled independence would lead to sociopathy. The limits of independence are set by ethics. Ethics are the rules about how to treat our environment including others. As such, they are filters through which potential actions must pass. Actions compared to the rules and found wanting should be prevented; all other actions are allowed. But ethics are about values. What kinds of actions are good? What sorts of actions are better? These are ethical questions that mean the individual's range of behavior is constrained by his first principles.

Ethics are, in part, an outgrowth of intelligence and empathy, but more than that, ethics are specifically an outgrowth of our values. However, the links between values, which are concepts, and ethics, manifested in behaviors or actions, are more of the nature of rubber bands than steel cables. Students may have different ethical behaviors connected to a shifting kaleidoscope of values and principles, but overwhelmingly the students in the classroom share the same core value system.

A student's ability to trace these connections is a function of the student's intelligence. As stated earlier, intelligence recognizes the possibility of conflict between values and makes sense of uncertainty, shading, complexity, and change. Absent intelligence, an individual's values become a list of "goods" and "bads," and ethics become merely good manners. Certainly good manners are useful, but a list is not a very good tool for navigating novel or unique ethical challenges.

Again, values and ethics are difficult to teach but easy to learn. Teachers will never be able to teach values or ethics by lecturing. A sound reason for not lecturing on values and ethics is the inherent danger. When a teacher is teaching values and ethics, he is walking through the single most dangerous minefield in all of education. Values and the ethical treatment of others are at the core of an individual's worldview. Look at the explosive, divisive, and passion-generating issues in our society. They are value-driven ethical issues about the treatment of others.

Perhaps the best way of teaching either values or ethics is through the use of stories; stories that arise in the classroom, history, or from the teacher's own life. In every case, especially the latter, the stories will only be effective to the extent that there is an element of trust present.

Ethics informs the kinds of interventions that students can make in their existence. If teachers are about increasing the historicity of their student, then teachers must be about values and ethics. If stories are a part of the curriculum, an education in ethics is a certainty.

ATTRIBUTES OF CHARACTER: LEADERSHIP

An individual with integrity, intelligence, and risk-taking may be able to intervene unilaterally in his own life to bring about really significant change. However, many, if not most, interventions require cooperation with others to accomplish, and therefore require empathy, ethics, common sense, and most important, leadership tempered with a willingness to serve.

Leadership seems to be like true love, difficult to define, but easy to recognize when you see it. The diversity of theories and styles of leadership based, for the most part, on anecdotal evidence or ideology is reflected in the thousands of leadership curricula found on the Web.

Relatively few schools have a formal course on leadership. If leadership is taught at all in the classroom, teachers have to do it along with the math, or French or English that they are actually hired to teach. This fact means that it is difficult to teach leadership, but, fortunately, does not make it difficult to learn. Students can learn leadership effectively by leading.

It is so simple; let students learn leadership and algebra by leading the class. Most teachers admit they never really knew and understood their subject until they had to teach it. It is equally true for students. Initially, the process is often painful, slow, and awkward, but students who lead will learn and understand far more completely than students who are led.

Except of course, it's not quite that simple. Leadership is scary. Leadership is precisely about taking a risk and being different. It has to be about having a vision of what needs to be done, communicating this vision, implementing strategies to accomplish these ends, and motivating others to join in the effort. There can be no certain recipe for leadership. In the details, it is always an intuitively creative act. This is a high-risk situation for a student because failure is rejection of the would-be leader. Such failure is expensive in the social capitals of status and self-image.

Be that as it may, every class has its leaders, independent of anything that the teacher has, or has not, done. The question is, are those leaders straight out of *Lord of the Flies*, or something else? Successful leadership is always about something else; the something else is a service component.

Effective leadership can only be created by its opposite, service. Service empowers others to intervene in their own lives to accomplish idiosyncratic goals while working on the common goals. The goals and desires of a leader are rarely exactly the same as the goals and desires of the followers. To the extent that the leader ignores these differences, his leadership is limited both in effectiveness and duration. Pretty soon the goals and desires of the others become paramount, and they wander away to do something else. The leader who will not serve must then resort to coercion or the threat of coercion. But coercion is not leadership.

Leadership cannot be taught by lecture. It can be taught by master teachers who have the trust of their students to create opportunities to lead, who provide a "safe zone" for the failure of leadership, and who have the compassion to empower student leaders to serve.

ATTRIBUTES OF CHARACTER: SERVICE

There is another kind of service, independent of leadership, that helps others to intervene in their own lives. This kind of service might be called "gift" service because it is given without an expectation of recompense or reciprocity. This kind of service, like leadership, requires empathy, ethics, common sense, and the willingness to take a risk. More important, absent independence and ethics, this kind of service becomes servitude.

Gift service requires action. Often, writing a check to an organization is not a gift service. Writing a check that seriously depletes your account may be a gift service to the extent you have to change your life as a result of that check. But more often, gift service is an action undertaken face-to-face with the recipient.

Opportunities for gift service abound in schools and classrooms but are notable for being unseen or ignored because, like leadership, this is scary stuff. Service is about taking a risk to be different from the recipient in having a vision of what might be done, communicating this vision to the recipient, and helping to accomplish these ends. Service is always an intuitively creative act. This is a high-risk situation for a student because it is a personal act. Failure is personal and expensive in the social capitals of status and self-image.

Master teachers see, and do not ignore, these opportunities for gift service because service freely given is an extraordinary teacher. To use a tired but useful cliché; the student has to walk a mile in another's shoes. By walking in the shoes or viewing through the eyes of another, the student may compare and contrast his own principles with those of another. It is difficult to imagine a student not increasing empathy, intelligence, and risk-taking and thereby increasing his own integrity in the course of providing gift service to another.

However, the teacher has to be very careful. Assigned or mandated gift service is an oxymoron; the student serves to satisfy the teacher.

The teachers' appropriate role is twofold. First, they have to make sure that the opportunities are explicit. In short, they have to point them out. Second, they have to tolerate a loss of control of the class. Precisely because service is intuitively creative, teachers cannot predict the exact form or timing. This does not mean that they have to tolerate shared answers to quizzes but they have to provide the freedom for students to interact, share, and help each other throughout the class in unexpected ways.

These sort of opportunities are generally ephemeral, and do not require a huge commitment on the part of the student. However, these are the moments where and when the students learn a great deal about themselves and what they are ready, willing, and able to commit to. The ability to commit to a gift service is that which makes us different from squirrels, and makes us fully human and fully alive.

ATTRIBUTES OF CHARACTER: SELF-CONFIDENCE

Self-confidence and self-knowledge are both the products and the sources of the other attributes of character. A necessary root of confidence is action. Confidence cannot arise from passivity. Action requires risk-taking, independence, and leadership or service. Action, combined with reflection, is experience and the basis for integrity, intelligence, empathy, and common sense, in addition to risk-taking, independence, and leadership or service.

Self-knowledge is the outcome of reflection using integrity, intelligence, empathy, and risk-taking. This kind of knowledge is made operational in statements such as, "This is who I am and this is what I know, can do, am interested in, and where I want to go." This kind of awareness is clearly the direct basis for self-confidence and the indirect basis for many of the other attributes of character.

Self-confidence and self-knowledge are goals of all teaching, but no teacher teaches them. They are generated within the student as a result of learning and practicing the other attributes of character. Each of the attributes of character—integrity tempered by empathy, intelligence tempered by awe, risk-taking tempered by common sense, independence tempered by ethics, leadership tempered by the desire to serve—play a role in the student's exercise of historicity. These attributes are also the foundation of the student's self-confidence and self-knowledge, which are the two best predictors of the student's ability to intervene successfully in his or her own life.

Master teachers have more than their share of these kinds of students precisely because they recognize that compassion, and the resultant trust, are a most important element in effective teaching. The teacher-student relationship is similar to that between two mountain climbers linked by a rope. Each retains a degree of freedom, but each must agree to climb, for one cannot, by brute strength alone, get two very far up the mountain. The teacher chooses the route, leads the effort, and anchors the line at difficult passages. However, the line must allow the student to choose alternative approaches and, on occasion, lead.

The line is woven of values and knowledge contributed by both. The teacher may start the process, but the student must help weave, tie, and maintain the line. Both the teacher and the student must have confidence in the line even when the other end cannot be seen or when the messages communicated are ambiguous and confusing.

If the line parts, the climb is over for the team. Before that point, the line can rescue the student who finds herself in a situation she cannot handle or bring the student up short of disaster if, through sheer exuberance, she leaps off the mountain and tries to fly.

Some lines allow for high plateaus and steep ascents. Some do not. The achievement of the climb is in the teacher and the student making the best possible use of the line to gain the highest possible level. The heart of the climb is in the interaction of the teacher and the student along the line in response to the mountain. No two climbs are ever the same: the teacher, the student, and the line have changed.

NOTES

1. A. Touraine, *The Self-production of Society* (Chicago: The University of Chicago Press, 1977).

2. A. Camus, *The Stranger*, trans. M. Ward (New York: Random House, 1988).

3. E. D. Hirsch, *Cultural Literacy* (Boston: Houghton Mifflin, 1987).

4. R. Fulgham, *All I Really Need to Know I Learned in Kindergarten* (New York: Ballantine Books, 2003).

5. Expeditionary learning has been developed by Outward Bound; see http://www.elob.org/.

6. The culture of performance is a major component of the curriculum at the Seattle Academy of Arts and Sciences; see http://www.seattleacademy.org/.

7. "Teenage Brain: A Work in Progress." Retrieved February 20, 2008, from http://www.nimh.nih.gov/publicat/teenbrain.cfm.

CHAPTER 3

How to Teach

REALLY GOOD TEACHING

Teachers who make a lifelong difference to their students do not teach algebra, art, French, science, or any other particular subject. Certainly, or at least I hope, we have all had outstanding, fascinating master teachers in one or more of these subjects. But do we remember them solely for the subject content? I would bet not. Rather we remember them because they changed us in some far more fundamental way

These teachers did not negate who or what we were although they may have negated some of our actions. They did not let us stay as we were; they used the subject to change us. And they never accepted the idea that learning the content was enough. They used the content as a springboard to the questions that really interested us: questions about us.

Master teachers have the competence, life experience, and compassion to achieve a tripartite goal of teaching content, increasing the student's capital by nurturing self-confidence and self-knowledge, and guiding the student's discovery of meaning in their life. In short, the teachers who made a lifelong difference to us did so by increasing, sometimes dramatically, our historicity.

The most remarkable thing about this whole process is that we, as students, allowed them to do this to us. In fact, although we were probably inarticulate in saying so, we craved it. Not because the process was easy; it generally was not. Not because we understood what was happening; I'm not sure we knew anything was happening. Most of us do not remember very many details of what was taught. What we remember is a connection built on trust, not between equals; we always knew who was in charge.

Although it was a mutual trust, the foundation was a trust first extended by the teacher based on a belief that, no matter how it seemed, we were living and doing the best we knew. This trust met us where we were with a confidence that empowered us to go beyond who we were, what we knew, and what we thought we could do.

Initially, we met this extended trust with distrust. Nobody had trusted us like this before except maybe our parents and sometimes not even them. But after a while, we met trust with trust and we gave as good as we got. We trusted with a confidence that allowed us to explore. We learned the content, but it was not always safe and accepted. We accrued internal and social capital through action. And more important, our worldview was shaken and our character shaped.

This kind of connection, relationship, or interaction between teacher and student is the single most powerful part of the student's school experience. Without this kind of relationship, schooling, at worst, is deadening drudgery and, at best, an exercise in mediocrity with little or no impact on the student's or society's historicity. Nothing the federal government, the state government, or the school district does will improve education and schooling nearly as much as recognizing the impact and magic created by a master teacher connecting with students.

TEACHING: THE FIRST CHALLENGE

The worldview of students in particular and the culture in general underwent an extraordinary transformation fifty or sixty years ago.[1] In less than two decades, this country transformed itself from a 70 percent rural population to a 70 percent urban population. This change has been reverberating throughout the society and the culture ever since, with impacts on all aspects of our lives.

The impact on education has been extensive, and has changed virtually every aspect of teaching. I will speak to only one; the idea that students are affected by a nature-deficit.[2] From the teacher's perspective, to the extent that students have a nature-deficit, there exists a challenge for teaching and learning.

The challenge arises because students are no longer immured in natural patterns and rhythms. Instead they are surrounded by, and immersed in, what appears to them to be a fragmented, unconnected, and asymmetric world. It is not my intention here to somehow romanticize the rural life. I've been there, and will not do that. Be that as it may, a rural existence tends to be innately more rhythmic, patterned, and connected than urban life. The sun comes up and the sun goes down, and a lot of life is connected to that fact: what and how much work is done, how much money is in the bank, and how available recreation or down time is.

In addition, rural youths frequently have a real role to play in both the family and the community. What they do, or do not do, makes a direct and measurable difference. In short, they may be more integrated into an adult world. In the urban setting, students tend to be far more isolated from the adult world. Generally they do not share in their parents' occupations, and they are far less frequently involved in the economic or social well-being of their parents.

The old model of teaching, with a focus on information and data transmission, was based, in part, on the assumption that the student was tightly connected to the context. It could be assumed that what was taught was useful almost immediately, and would be reinforced by direct experience. These days, once the teacher leaves the basics of reading, writing, and arithmetic, the information has only a tenuous connection with the student's immediate context. Much of what is taught in high school biology these days was taught in graduate school not long ago. It cannot be seen or touched, and must be taken on faith, nor is it relevant to a student's immediate existence. The same is probably true for much of the rest of the curriculum as well.

Under these circumstances, from the student perspective, going to school for any purpose other than social makes little or no sense. How in the ever-loving world is a teacher supposed to keep them involved, interested, and focused on content?

TEACHING: THE SECOND CHALLENGE

A second culture change has been accelerating since about fifty years ago as a result of the development of technology in general and television in particular. In 1966, Marshal McLuhan wrote:

> Today, the ordinary child lives in an electronic environment. He lives in a world of information overload. From infancy, he is confronted with the television image. . . . Any moment of television provides more data than could be recorded in a dozen pages of prose. The next moment provides more pages of prose. The children, so accustomed to a "Niagara of data" in their ordinary environments, are introduced to nineteenth-century classrooms and curricula, where data flow is not only small in quantity but fragmented in pattern. The subjects are unrelated. The environmental clash can nullify motivation in learning.[3]

The preceding was written when a student's "connectivity" was limited to a passive reception of radio, television, and the printed page. In addition, a student might have a participatory connection via a landline phone, face-to-face conversations, and, again, the printed page. If the data flow was a "Niagara" in 1966, how would you describe it these days with hundreds of on-demand cable channels, broadband links, ubiquitous wi-fi, multitasking cell phones, and iPods?

Perhaps the best description is as a phantasmagoria, or, "A fantastic sequence of haphazardly associative imagery, as seen in dreams or fever."[4] But whatever you call it, the data stream inundating students is a tremendous challenge to teachers. They cannot compete. Or, more accurately, teachers cannot compete as long as they offer "nineteenth-century classrooms and curricula" in a fragmented fashion. So what is a teacher to do?

First, the teacher has to focus, not so much on discrete information, but on patterns. It is not enough to give students a catalogue of fascinating information. The information the teacher can present will have a tough time competing on the fascination factor with all the other information coming at the student. But if the teacher deals with generalized patterns, what is taught is more likely to be relevant to the student's life outside of school.

Second, the teacher should use technology but not the way it has been used. Most teachers have students use a computer as a smart typewriter, a large file cabinet, a huge library, or a slow telephone. Very few teachers use technology to teach students a new way of thinking.

Third, the teacher has to create an educational structure that fits the culture of the student population. In many, if not most, classrooms, the educational content and structure have not changed significantly since before World War II. But the American culture has undergone paroxysms of change since the 1960s and 1970s. These changes have not been just about content but, equally, about structural relationships. For many students, going to school is tantamount to going to a foreign country.

TEACHING: GENERAL SYSTEMS THEORY

If the teacher wishes to increase a student's historicity, the most direct way of doing so is to help the student in assigning meaning to the flow of information swirling around him. The first step in assigning meaning is to organize or classify the information in some way.

Wurman[5] argues that, "The ways of organizing information are finite. It can only be organized by location, alphabet, time, category, or hierarchy." These can be used simultaneously. Thus you could organize information about vehicles by type (category), where made (location), and expense (hierarchy).

However, while organization may be a necessary first step; it is not sufficient for the assignment of anything more than the most rudimentary meaning. The meaning of information comes from its relationship to other information to form or change patterns. For example, adding one more M&M to a student's bag of M&Ms has little or no meaning. But adding a loose ruby to the bag of M&Ms is meaningful. Why is it meaningful? Because it changes the relationships between the M&Ms and the student. No longer are all the things in the bag the same kind. No longer are they all benign; they might break a tooth. The information about a ruby has meaning, but not just because it's a ruby. A pebble could have the same meaning.

Information has meaning only to the extent that it changes the recipient. It can change the recipient only if it interacts with other information to change a pattern the recipient already has. A second example could be a piece of music that the student listens to. If the music does not change the student's relationship to the class of things called "music" in some way, then the piece of music has no meaning outside of its membership in the class, "music." If it has no greater meaning, then it may safely be ignored or forgotten.

A generalized and perhaps fundamental description of pattern formation and change is found in General Systems Theory which is about the flow, impact, and transformation of information. A system is an organization of elements, parts, subsystems, variables, or entities interacting in such a way that the outcome of the interaction is not predictable directly from the characteristics of the elements or parts. In short, a system is more than the sum of its parts. It is dynamic, characterized by the interactions rather than its parts. For example, one adult in a room with a group of students does not define the system. The flows of information determine whether the room is an after-school detention, a classroom, or something else entirely.

An example of a system is the student's historicity. Historicity has three subsystems: knowledge, capital, and worldview interacting to produce an intervention in the student's life that cannot be specified, a priori, directly from the student's knowledge base, social or fiscal capital, nor worldview. The intervention is not the product of one or even all of the subsystems, but rather the interactions between the subsystems. And the interactions are all about information flows among knowledge, capital, and worldview.

If the goal is to increase the student's historicity, then teaching must have a focus of helping the student think about the role information plays in controlling and transforming the systems of which we are all a part.

TEACHING: SYSTEMS THINKING

It is easy to say that teaching should help students think about the role information plays in controlling and transforming systems. But what does the word "think" mean?

> Thinking . . . we all do it. But what is it? The dictionary says it's "to have a thought; to reason, reflect on, or ponder." Does that clear it up for you? It didn't for me. I will define thinking as consisting of two activities: constructing mental models, and then simulating them in order to draw conclusions and make decisions. . . . What the heck is a mental model? It's a "selective abstraction" of reality that you create and then carry around in your head. As big as some of our heads get, we still can't fit reality in there. Instead, we have models of various aspects of reality. We simulate these models in order to "make meaning" out of what we're experiencing, and also to help us arrive at decisions that inform our actions.[6]

Although we have never used the term before, much of what has been written so far concerns students' mental models. The mental models that the student carries around in his or her head are the student's reality. The foundational mental model is the worldview that gives meaning to life and the interventions we make to change or create our existence. A worldview is an individual's principles and ideas about the nature of Self, Others, the Universe, Knowledge, Truth, and Value. These ideas are generally unconscious and unexamined and sometimes incoherent or self-contradictory, but all the information that comes to the student is processed in light of these models and provides a basis for an individual's perceiving, thinking, doing, and valuing.

General Systems Theory and, less formally, systems thinking, provide a language and an approach to making this processing more explicit and more discussable. "Systems thinking . . . involves an awareness and understanding of mental models and the importance of surfacing and clarifying our own mental models and the mental models of others in order to effectively communicate."[7]

Most folks have mental models that equate phrases such as "systems thinking" and "model simulation" with technology and computers. Most systems thinking can be (and actually is) done without any involvement of computers or any technology more advanced than paper and pencil. It is true that there is a myriad of software packages that support systems thinking and model simulations, but none of that is an absolute requirement.

Neither is systems thinking limited to the sciences or mathematics. Systems happen. Systems happen in all disciplines. Some systems are purely symbolic in nature and exist only as mental constructs. These are cognitive systems and worldview is one of them. There are systems that are partially symbolic and partially substantive. These are by far the most common, and they exist in all disciplines including history, language, the arts, and the sciences. What this means is that English teachers, art teachers, physics teachers, and calculus teachers can all speak the same language to their students.

TEACHING: SYSTEMS THINKING 2

What sets systems thinking apart from analytical thinking is that it starts off in a different direction. The more traditional, reductionist, analytic approach is to break a system apart to characterize the individual bits and pieces. It is a valuable way of looking at the world because it draws boundaries, isolates, and allows a degree of focus that otherwise would be impossible. Reductionism has made possible an almost incomprehensible explosion of knowledge since the Renaissance.

Systems thinking, in contrast, puts the bits and pieces into context and examines the interactions and relations within that context. Instead of looking at progressively smaller and perhaps simpler units, systems thinking looks at progressively larger, possibly more complex, units searching for commonalities and isomorphisms that might be found in many kinds of systems.

A commonality seen from the systems viewpoint is the possibility of emergent properties. Emergent properties are properties of the system as a whole that are not inherent in the bits and pieces themselves, but rather develop in the interactions of one with another. For example, there is an immutable law in biology that states all cells come from cells. If somebody wished to build a simple bacterial cell, analytically it would be possible to learn every bit and piece that constituted a particular bacterium. It would take time and work, but it is a certainty that it could be done. It is equally certain that all that time and work would never lead to the creation of a live bacterium. Life is an emergent property; life is not inherent in the bits and pieces themselves. Life is found in the interactions between all those bits and pieces. Until we understand those interactions and relations within the bacterial context, life will only come from life.

A second commonality of systems is the ability to maintain identity based on the existence of feedback loops. Naturally occurring, substantive systems do something. They do not just sit there. In fact, most natural systems do a dizzying array of things simultaneously. All of this activity requires an ongoing input of material, energy, or information from the environment. As a general rule, sources of such inputs are variable. Any system existing over time must maintain its structure and function in the face of variable inputs of material, energy, or information. Feedback loops allow the system to monitor its performance, and respond with a structural or functional change to maintain its identity in the face of short-term, environmental change.

Both commonalities are found in the attributes of an individual's character. Self-confidence and self-knowledge are both the products, and the sources, of the other attributes of character. A necessary input to confidence is action. But any action taken is shaped by the attributes of character. Equally, any action taken will shape the very attributes that shaped it. Action and the attributes of character are linked together by multiple, complex feedback loops; they are mutually causal.

None of the attributes of character act alone. All are intertwined in complex relationships resulting, finally, in a transformation of one kind of thing, action, into another kind of thing, self-confidence or self-knowledge. But the details of the action, self-confidence, or self-knowledge are the result of the interactions, rather than in the attributes themselves.

THE SYSTEMS CLASSROOM: WHAT IT IS NOT

So how does a teacher translate systems thinking into the classroom? There is no one answer. Show me ten classrooms where systems thinking holds sway, and I will show you ten very different classrooms. But what about some of the classroom models where systems thinking does not happen?

The first such model has the teacher as the physical, intellectual, or psychological pivot point for all that happens. A teacher-centric class cannot be based on systems thinking; the complexity of the class is denied. There are way too many inputs, elements, interactions, and outputs whose existence are denied or ignored.

Most of what the students bring to the class is ignored. It is expected that the students come to class ready, primed, and receptive to whatever it is that the teacher offers; they are blank slates upon which the teacher is to write. The focus is on teaching, not learning. With the teacher as the pivot point, student-student interaction is constrained. The interactions that count are the student-teacher interactions rather than student-student or student-material interactions.

Because the focus is on teaching rather than learning, the elements of feedback are seriously truncated. The flow of information from the teacher to the student dwarfs the flow from the student to the teacher. The measure of success is regurgitation. Can the student give back what was given? Yes? No? Success? Failure?

Taken to an extreme, such a classroom would be a nightmare. The model of teacher-as-pivot is not all that successful. It might have worked in an earlier time, when students were viewed as being more interchangeable, and the curriculum less advanced, but it hasn't been in vogue since Sputnik. This model still exists but it is viewed in the same light as an embarrassing relative, acknowledged but not to be discussed.

The model that replaced teacher-as-pivot was essentially the text-as-pivot. After Sputnik, the teacher-as-pivot was viewed as a failure; the general opinion was that the teachers were responsible for letting the country down. Rather than fire everybody, an effort was made to write textbooks that were fail-safe recipes for teaching, but not necessarily for learning. Again, the weakness of a single pivot model is manifest. Everything that is wrong in the first model is wrong with the second. In addition, there is a new weakness. The perfect biology text-as-pivot would be substantially different in New York City and North Dakota because what students in those places bring to the classroom is substantially different. But the text cannot address those differences, nor grant significance to those differences. There can be no "place-based education" using a text-as-pivot model.

A third classroom model is now being imposed on classrooms, the test-as-pivot. If anything this model is the most insidious of all. It imposes a structure and an outcome from the outside environment rather from inside the classroom. In doing so, it can, and does, ignore any and all inputs, elements, interactions, and outputs that might be part of a classroom. In this model, not only are students nonentities, so are classrooms, schools, and communities. Only one interaction counts, and it is not the student-student, student-teacher, or student-material interaction. It is the isolated student interacting with the test that counts. This is equally true whether the test is the result of the NCLB, the IB, SAT, ACT, or the AP. Multiple-guess tests and systems thinking are incompatible.

More important, it is a trivial system indeed that returns an input as output with no change. How trivial are we going to make education and our students?

THE SYSTEMS CLASSROOM: WHAT IT IS

If the historic and predominant classroom models are counterproductive to systems thinking, what kind of model would be more amenable to systems thinking?

The answer to this question cannot be presented as a recipe. Rather the answer has to be presented as a direction to be traveled. To begin, the systems-based classroom will focus on: the whole rather than the parts; the interactions rather than the pieces or parts; process rather than structure; networks rather than hierarchies; and nonlinear rather than linear causality. Second, the classroom will have multiple pivot points including, but not limited to, the teacher, the curriculum contents, the individual students, and important inputs from the environment. Third, the classroom will have porous boundaries. Learning will not stop at disciplinary boundaries, nor will it stop at the classroom or school walls. And last, an explicit element of the curriculum will be to look for, and at, patterns that occur and recur throughout the class activities.

So what does such a classroom or curriculum actually look like?

- A major focus is on the development and support of a few "enduring ideas" that will stick with the students when they have long forgotten the teacher's name.
- Emergent properties will be a coin of the realm.
- A movie rather than a photograph will be the metaphor for student discussions and explanations.
- Teacher-student and student-student alliances to make progress will be dynamic and shifting dependent on needs, capabilities, and interests.
- Explanations will include a broad range of causal relationships and interactions including those more distant and those more immediate, exogenous and endogenous.
- On any given day, any one of several elements—teacher, text, subject, or better yet, the students—may serve as the primary pivot-point.
- There will be recognition that more is unknown than known about most, if not all, students.
- There will be recognition that students bring to any class a wealth of knowledge that can serve to move the class forward.
- Multiple sources of information, rather than a single text, will be in play including teachers, students, the community, the broader environment, and other disciplines.
- People from outside the classroom and the school will serve as resources for the class.
- Students will spend time outside of the classroom learning from and applying their knowledge to the broader environment.
- And finally, facts are not the be-all and end-all for the educational process. The sine qua non is how those facts fit into patterns developed both in the class and borrowed from other disciplines.

This sort of classroom becomes dynamic and complex. But then, rich, effective, classrooms are dynamic, complex systems in and of themselves. As such, they are a fitting foundation for teaching and learning systems thinking.

THE SYSTEMS CLASSROOM: COCKEYED OPTIMIST

The systems thinking classroom is only going to develop under the aegis of a master teacher with competence, life experience, and compassion. If the teacher lacks any of these attributes, the chances of a systems thinking classroom developing are somewhere between slim and none and Slim just left town. But not every master teacher can or does develop such a classroom. Perhaps two closely related, general personality traits are needed: enthusiasm and flexibility.

Teachers with the needed enthusiasm have been described as being cockeyed optimists "who routinely have higher perceptions of psychological and physical well-being because they are more action-oriented, more effective at coping with stress, more willing to confront, more likely to put a situation in the best possible light, and more able to grow personally from difficult experiences."[8]

Optimistic teachers are confident that the world can be changed. However, they do not believe that only they have the power to change the world. They trust their students. Therefore, their role is not that of a blacksmith hammering a piece into shape, but rather a gardener encouraging growth. "Implicit in such views are the assumptions that everyone has the power to be creative and powerful, that new ideas exist, and that riddles can be solved."[9]

A second trait of optimistic teachers is the belief that they have never peaked as a teacher. What happened in their class yesterday can be improved on. It has never been as good as it might be. They are constantly looking for other ways to do things, to broaden the experience, to enrich the information sources, and to tailor the structure and function of the class to meet student needs and interests.

Another way of saying much the same thing is to say that the cockeyed optimist is convinced that just around the hill or on the other side of the fence there is a hidden treasure worth going to find. Such teachers constantly push the boundaries and explore new paths and new ways of doing things.

The other side of this optimism is flexibility. Optimistic teachers are never satisfied with the status quo. They will set out to find a better way, which inherently means change, and often means uncertainty about exactly what will happen next. The optimistic teacher starts every year, every class, every lesson without knowing exactly how it will end up. There are too many potential branch points. No matter how sharp the plan, the variety represented by the students means there will always be unknowns that appear in the implementation.

Being in the classroom of this kind of optimistic teacher is a little like whitewater rafting with a competent guide. You know where you are going, but the details of how you get there are open to change and adventure. The smallest change in the inputs can generate a dramatic difference in trajectory. If you expect any two trips to be the same or even to successfully follow a plan, you are doomed to be frustrated. But flexibility is not particularly heroic to the optimist. After all, it's all going to work out for the best, right?

THE SYSTEMS CLASSROOM: BUT NOT CRAZY

As I read what I have written about the systems thinking classroom, and the kind of teacher who guides it, I'm afraid that I've left an image of a crazy, mad-hatter sort of person swinging from the light fixtures, bouncing off the window sills, contributing to the phantasmagoria that is life, and adding to the students' confusion.

It's true that a confident, or cockeyed, optimist is going to have a class that is less predictable and less formulaic. It's true that this teacher is open to changing course in midstream, seeing what is working, or not, and changing things to make them work better. It is true that this is a teacher who will introduce new elements into the class even when the outcome is uncertain. It is true that this is a teacher willing to let the students on occasion lead and is comfortable with the kinds of ambiguity that are involved.

All of these statements are true, but this is no wild-eyed pied-piper leading students away, at least not if this is a master teacher. Master teachers are competent, have life experience, and are compassionate.

Their competence means that no matter what happens in class they can always navigate their way to the central point they wish to make. Competence means that no matter which side road is taken, they know the subject well enough to get back to the highway. The take-home message for the students will be as planned. In addition, competence has to be based on rationality. There may be flights of fancy in the process, but the underlying structure is not random or irrational. The underlying rationale is explainable. Going back to the image of whitewater rafting, no matter how unpredictable the path down the river, water never runs uphill.

Master teachers' life experience means that they understand that nobody can maintain a frenetic pace for very long. Pause and reflection are an integral part of any experience and the basis for learning. Absent pause and reflection, there is no meaning. The goal of the master teacher is to assist in the assignment of meaning. Therefore, the class will not be an ongoing carnival ride of swoops and dips with radical changes in direction. There will be periods of looking back and seeing where the class has been, what has really been learned, and how it all might fit together.

Their compassion means that they can meet the students where they are. In practice this means that, using the river metaphor again, students will not be thrown out of the raft to make their own way. They will travel with the relative stability of the raft under them, and they will have a guide at all times helping them get through the rough places. They will not hit the rocks without padding and protection. And if they do get thrown out of the raft, the guide has made sure they have a life jacket and a helmet so no serious damage is done.

The master teachers who are also systems thinkers are curious autodidacts ranging freely and widely across the intellectual terrain looking at elements, ideas, facts, patterns, and perspectives that will change them. But they are first and foremost master teachers unwilling to leave their students behind. The well-being of their students is paramount, and that fact puts limits on where they go and how they get there.

THE SYSTEMS CLASSROOM: TECHNOLOGY

The second response that master teachers can make to the challenges posed by the extraordinary cultural changes of the last fifty years is to use the development of computer power and the Internet or World Wide Web in a more effective manner.

At the moment there are two major perspectives on how to teach: the instructivist and the constructivist perspectives. These perspectives can be summarized as follows.

> The older "instructivist" perspectives on learning tend to regard knowledge as a substance in the mind of individuals that is independent of context, to view learning as an activity for the individual, and to reductively structure learning in terms of the gradual accumulation of pieces of information. . . . In contrast, recent socio-cognitive or "constructivist" perspectives regard knowledge as an emerging characteristic of activities taking place among individuals in specific contexts, to view learning as a developmental process occurring first in an interpersonal domain (i.e., socio-cognitive or between people) and later in an intrapersonal domain (i.e., cognitively or within an individual), and to recognize that learning is a constructive activity that often requires active and substantial reorganization of existing conceptual structures.[10]

To date, computer power and the Internet have been used by educators primarily as a management tool or to support the instructivist perspective on teaching. And there is nothing wrong with this use. Computerized attendance, grading, communicating, and generally tracking students is a huge savings of time. As classes get larger and demands get greater, this use of the computer may be the difference between surviving and crashing in flames.

In terms of instruction, the use of the computer and the Web to enlarge the school's library, to supplement or update a text with Web-sites or Web-quests, to import specialized faculty and courses, to organize, assign, receive, and revise assignments, is a blessing for educators committed to meeting the needs of a wide variety of students.

Be that as it may, none of the efforts listed inherently change the instructivist model of education. It allows that model to work more efficiently and more effectively. After all, we could have done all of the above fifty years ago if we had the time, the money, and the energy. It did not happen simply because nobody was willing to expend that level of resources.

More important, what is not happening is that the computer is not being used to change the way that teachers and students think. The computer has the inherent ability to let people communicate and explore the implications of complex, tentative explanations, hypotheses, and ideas quickly and easily; for example, Second Life.[11] As individuals, working at a less comprehensive level of simulation, both students and teachers can create and explore the implications of various models of how the world works. In short, we have not effectively explored the capacity of the computer when linked with the Internet to support a constructivist model of education.

THE SYSTEMS CLASSROOM: USING MODELS

At the core of the constructivist perspective on learning is the idea that the student must be an active partner, constructing his knowledge base, and interacting with the stream of information to add value by constructing a web of meaning. Constructivist learning requires action and change on the part of the learner. But not just any action; recitation, repetition, regurgitation, and mimicry do not count as constructivist learning.

A way of understanding constructivist learning is to focus on the student's mental models. Mental models are representations of how the world works. These models can be developed vicariously, especially for young children, based on stories or myths and interactions with and observations of adults. As individuals get older, stories and myths remain important, but direct experience gains importance and is often deemed more trustworthy. After all, will eighteen-year-olds really believe what you say, that is, a story, rather than what they experience? Some of the characteristics of mental models pertaining to learning are:

- They are incomplete and constantly evolving.
- They are usually not accurate representations of a phenomenon; they typically contain errors and contradictions.
- They are parsimonious and provide simplified explanations of complex phenomena.
- They often contain measures of uncertainty about their validity that allow them to be used even if incorrect.[12]

Whenever information is received, it flows into the student's mental models. Most often this is an additive process. The incoming information simply confirms the mental model. Because models are predictive in the sense that if "this happens" now, "that happens" next, the student can respond to the incoming information in an appropriate manner. This process is basically an enriched behaviorist model of stimulus-response behavior patterns or, even more simply, habituation.

It can be argued that, while mental models are clearly learned at some point, if the incoming information does not alter the extant model, no learning is taking place now. If the information does not fit or reinforce the extant model, the information is often denied in the sense that it is simply deemed wrong, misapprehended, or incomplete.

However models are not static. If the information is wrong, misapprehended, or incomplete often enough, change in the model will happen.

Constructs [models] are used for predictions of things to come, and the world keeps rolling along and revealing these predictor [sic] to be either

correct or misleading. This fact provides the basis for revision of constructs and, eventually, of whole construction systems. If it were a static
world that we lived in, our thinking about it might be static too.[13]

Most often the change in the models is a fine-tuning of structure
or connection. Sometimes, change comes in a "Eureka" moment, a
sudden insight, an epiphany, or a catharsis where the old is destroyed
and replaced almost instantaneously.

If it happens with a smile, these are the moments teachers live for.
They are rare but oh so wonderful. So the question has to be, how
does one encourage them? The short answer is the teacher helps the
student make his model explicit.

THE SYSTEMS CLASSROOM: A MODEL

A very rudimentary model might look something like figure 3.1, below. The most common way to make these kinds of models explicit
is to ask questions such as, "What are the causes of X, Y, or Z?" The
easy way to answer this kind of question is to develop a causal loop
model of cause and effect. For example, if the question were, what
are the variables that control a student's academic success, an answer might be presented as follows:[14]

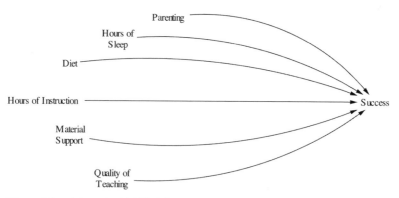

Figure 3.1.   *A Laundry-List Model.*

We can argue about what else should be on the list of variables, but that is not the point. All models are incomplete and to some degree incorrect. The question to ask is, is this model in some way useful?

And the answer is yes, precisely because we can talk about what should be included on the left side of the model to make explicit our ideas about what controls student success. If we can get agreement, we will have some explicit understanding of the system that produces student success.

This kind of model is "the laundry list model of causation" useful for answering questions such as, "What were the causes of World War I?" Or "How do you define life?" Or "Where and when do you use a semicolon?" A laundry list model may be a perfectly reasonable way of thinking about the last question but it would be limiting for the first two.

In the above model, causality is unidirectional from left to right. According to this model, the system underlying student success operates on a strictly feed-forward, open-loop basis. The implication of such a structure is that student success is dependent on the starting conditions. If any of the initial variables are lacking, the student is doomed. However, if one, or more, of the variables is at the optimum value, the student may have success.

This model is woefully incomplete, but the more important point seems to be that it does not reflect either how the real world works or the complexity of the mental models most teachers have about student success. Every teacher knows of students who have risen above the most onerous inputs and succeeded gloriously and others who have arrived with golden inputs and accomplished little.

THE SYSTEMS CLASSROOM: A BETTER MODEL

A more useful model might look something like figure 3.2.

This model says everything the previous model said, but has included significantly richer kinds of information. For instance, parenting, however defined, is both directly and indirectly linked to

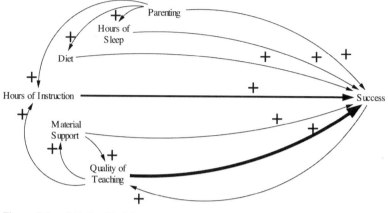

Figure 3.2.   *A Better Model.*

success, through attendance, hours of sleep, and diet. The previous model suggested that the quality of teaching affects success. In this model there is an additional feedback loop; the level of success directly affects the quality of teaching, and, indirectly, attendance, and material support, which, in turn, affect success.

The addition of a positive sign by each arrow indicates that the linked variables are positively correlated; they move in the same direction. An improvement in quality of teaching will cause an increase in student success. A reduction in quality will reduce success. A negative sign would indicate a negative correlation; the linked variables would move in opposite directions.

By changing the weight of the arrows, we can indicate the relative importance of the causes of success. The quality of teaching and hours of instruction are the two most important factors in the student's success. No distinction has been made between the remaining factors.

There are two advantages to this type of causal loop model. First the only technology required is paper and pencil. If the student can draw, the student can benefit from drawing a model such as this. What is important here is not whether this model is correct or not. At best, it is a tentative hypothesis. What is important is that the model gives us a starting point for talking about the system at hand. As the model becomes more explicit, it becomes easier to have a conversation about the model's structure, and to describe how it is different from our own. These differences trigger questions, focus discussions, and guide our thinking about the system.

The second advantage of this type of model is that it supports student learning, exploration, and questioning at multiple levels; in short, the model can grow with the student's understanding. The initial model may be a unidirectional, post hoc propter hoc laundry list containing a few obvious proximal causes of an effect. As the student's understanding deepens, broadens, and becomes more sophisticated, the model will extend to more distal causation woven into multiple, more complex, feedback loops. This kind of model can be like a favorite teddy bear. As time passes, it loses its shiny newness, but gains meaning at all the wear points.

THE SYSTEMS CLASSROOM: INTRODUCTION TO SIMULATIONS

Causal loop models can be very useful in class. They provide a structure for learning about a broad range of topics. A classroom discussion of the causes of World War I can move from a discussion of unidirectional, laundry-list causality to a richer understanding of the interactions that brought about an assassination and a war. A discussion of *Animal Farm*, *Macbeth*, or *Charlotte's Web* can be explored in terms of feedback loops and interdependent, change-over-time interactions. In the sciences, these kinds of models can be used to help students understand homeostasis in natural systems such as the maintenance of body temperature or the maintenance of chemical equilibria.

While a causal loop model implies a certain dynamism in a system, it cannot specify the details about the interactions that link the system together. Those details must be presented elsewhere, in explanatory discussions or paragraphs. It would be a wonderful thing if those explanations could be incorporated into the model itself; that is, if each arrow could be described by a logical, detailed statement. If they were, the model could be "run" as a simulation to see how the actual system might function or to compare the functioning of the model with the functioning of the system.

The downside of the increased power of the "runnable" model is that simulation pretty much requires a computer.[15] You cannot run a simulation in any meaningful way with pencil and paper. On the other hand, the advantages of having simulations include the abilities to try out alternative scenarios on the model before they occur in the real system, to learn how the system might respond to the different scenarios, and, on that basis, to learn how to intervene more effectively in one's own existence; that is, how to exercise one's own historicity.

If students could build useful simulation models of some parts of their lives, they would own a set of very powerful tools for effectively managing their own existence. Building such a model is not always easy. It may be like learning a new language; earlier is easier than later. And it requires the student to practice some new skill sets.

The first new skill set required is a sort of "split vision," where the students have to keep their eyes on the details of the model while simultaneously standing back to see the overall structure. In many classes, students are required to stand back and speak in generalities. In other classes, students look through the metaphorical microscope to understand the details in a small field of vision. In building a simulation, the students have to look though the microscope at the details of the interactions while, at the same time, watching the rest of the model to see the effects of those details.

The second required skill set students must have when building simulation models is the ability to recognize, accept, and respond effectively to the limits of their models. If models were totally complete and realistic, they would not be models; they would be reality. All models are, perforce, incomplete and unrealistic, and, therefore, are uncertain at best and incorrect at worst. If students are to successfully intervene in their lives, they need to plan for the uncertainty and error in all the models they use; even the models that are part of their worldview.

A RUNNABLE MODEL ILLUSTRATED

Using a Runnable Model

Figure 3.3 shows a dynamic Stella model illustrating overshoot where "A" is a resource with a fixed replacement rate, and "B" is a

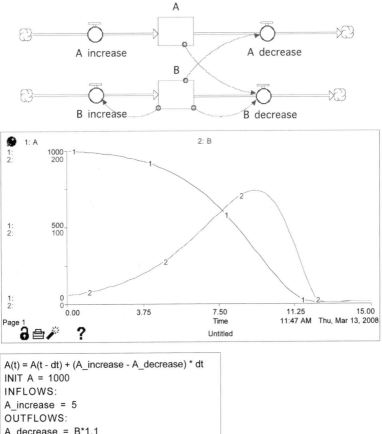

```
A(t) = A(t - dt) + (A_increase - A_decrease) * dt
INIT A = 1000
INFLOWS:
A_increase = 5
OUTFLOWS:
A_decrease = B*1.1
B(t) = B(t - dt) + (B_increase - B_decrease) * dt
INIT B = 10
INFLOWS:
B_increase = B*.5
OUTFLOWS:
B_decrease = B*(B/A)
```

Figure 3.3.   A Runnable Model Illustrated.

population of consumers. In the real world, this model might represent a population of rabbits in a fenced field of grass or wells drawing on an oil field. There are three parts to the model: a map of the system, the equations specifying how the system works, and a graph showing changes in "A" and "B" over time.

If I were a teacher introducing this model in a class of novices, I would first identify "A" as grass in a fenced field and "B" as the rabbit population of the field. I would then ask the students, based on the graph, what happens to the rabbits and the grass over time? No problem, all of my students would be able to present a coherent and acceptable answer. After all, this is "way too easy." But then I would ask them what part of the model causes that effect? It would require some discussion, but eventually, they would come to the conclusion that the answer is not a single bit or piece, but the interaction of all the bits and pieces that generate that pattern.

The next step is to have the students play with the model. They can try experiments that change the values and structures of the equations to see what happens next. Perhaps they double the birth rate of the rabbits or they start with half as much grass and a quarter as many rabbits. They can add new elements to the model. Perhaps there is a rabbit plague every two years that kills half the rabbits. What happens then? And finally, it is possible to build a model where rabbits and grass remain in equilibrium?

Once students are comfortable with this model, I would broaden the discussion to questions of where else it might be found, in students' lives, in history, in economics, and in the arts, and so on. The discussions are priceless in terms of generating an understanding of patterns and isomorphisms in apparently diverse events. This understanding allows students to recognize how common this pattern is, while forcing them to recognize subtle but meaningful differences between occurrences. In short, this simple model can increase student understanding of how the world works and it provides a cross-disciplinary structure without blurring the details.

However, this model is not The Unified Theory of Everything. There is much for which it is not germane. For other applications, we might need other, widely applicable, relatively simple, generic models. A series of such models, explanations, and applications can be found, often downloaded, in the professional development materials produced by MIT, and available from the Clexchange.[16] Generic models can be used to understand a wide range of real-world situations and they can be used to give meaning to a huge amount of material covered in broad range of courses. But again, they are inherently limited because they are relatively simple. A reasonable analogy is that each is a sentence in a world that needs paragraphs. But like sentences they can be put together to form paragraphs. Complex systems can be described by using simple generic models as building blocks.

Putting the sentences into meaningful paragraphs is a skill like learning a new language, easiest when young. Systems thinking and modeling have been successfully introduced in the very early grades.[17] Imagine the positive impact of fluency on the historicity of students.

LIMITATIONS OF A RUNNABLE MODEL

I wish that using the systems approach to develop a fluency in the use of models was an educational panacea. It is not. The classroom is too complex a system for that to be true; there can be no single recipe for success. A significant percentage of students resist this approach and simply want to know what's going to be on the test. After all, these days in too many test-centric classes, the expectation is that the teacher lectures; students take notes; perhaps do a worksheet or two; and then give it all back on a test.

That pattern does not totally disappear in the systems classroom. After all, no model can be built in a vacuum. The teacher still has to help provide a foundation on which the student can build on, and has to provide a degree of guidance and evaluation, where evaluation is going to run the gamut of tests, rubrics, presentations, and other appropriate means.

Some folks believe that student-built models will not change things very much at all.

> Educators have become more clever and imaginative in the teaching models employed, and it is not uncommon to see teachers using approaches such as discovery learning, simulations, cooperative learning, inquiry training, problem-centered learning, concept learning, and a host of variations on these basic models. More recent approaches include simulated problem solving through the use of interactive video discs and computer programs. Some of these approaches certainly make learning more active and enjoyable than traditional, content-based deductive learning, but the "bottom line" is that there are certain predetermined bodies of information and thinking processes that students are expected to acquire. The instructional effects of the deductive model are those directly achieved by leading the learner in prescribed directions.[18]

Unfortunately, this is correct. Systems thinking, model building, and simulation may be simply new, constructivist clothes for an old corpse. They are better clothes than it is presently wearing, better made, more effective in meeting the onslaughts of the environment, more acceptable, and useful in a broad range of situations, and just plain more stylish; but to the extent that it is totally instructivist, deductive in the above quote, the body they clothe is pretty moribund.

Systems thinking, model building, and simulation will only reach their potential as learning tools when they are then incorporated into a vibrant process that is both inductive and deductive, teacher lead and student lead, disciplinary and trans-disciplinary, rigorous and fun, and most important, safe and adventurous.

CURRICULUM DESIGN

In the beginning of this chapter, I suggested that there were three ways that teachers could adapt to the cultural changes of the last fifty to sixty years. First, the teacher has to focus, not so much on discrete information, but on patterns. It is not enough to give students a catalogue of fascinating information. The information the teacher can present will have a tough time competing on the fascination factor with all the other information coming at the student. But if the teacher deals with generalized patterns, what is taught is more likely to be relevant to the student's life outside of school.

Second, use technology, not just as a smart typewriter, a large file cabinet, a huge library, or a slow telephone. Instead, use the technology to support systems thinking, model building, and simulation.

The third suggestion, that the teacher has to create an educational structure that fits the culture of the student population, is where we can breathe life into education.

> What had been the unsung glory of the American approach to education—something never measured in those international tests (on which U.S. youths score so badly)—is the way a tradition of open class discussion has fostered free thinking and rambunctious argumentativeness. And yes, confident creativity, to some degree. (At least among the upper half of students.)
>
> And here's a startling irony that illustrates the point. While we rush, rather thoughtlessly, to copy the rote memorization techniques that enable kids in Asia and elsewhere to score so well on standardized tests, the education ministries in Japan, China, and India are frantically dispatching minions into the field, exhorting teachers to "teach in a more American fashion," in order to stop squelching the creativity, imagination, and argumentative confidence that we encourage (or used to encourage) so well.[19]

Further, if we can breathe life into this process we call schooling it will be because we challenge our students' present models through experience that addresses their lives in the here and now. The operative phrase here is "challenge experience." Students rarely change their mental models based on information passively received. Yes, mental models can change dramatically if the received information is heavily laden with emotional content. But one hopes that that kind of information transfer does not happen too often at school.

To the extent that students are interested in, involved with, responsive to, and actively creating their experience in school, students' thinking can be challenged and changed by their experience. But it is important to note that the change is generated by the student in response to his or her experience, and not brought about directly by the teacher or the curricular content.

These two ideas are merely pleasant bromides unless we can in some way translate them into a practice that moves away from the deductive, prescribed, education towards an authentic, performance, and life-based exercise.

There are hundreds of school and education reform models available for consideration. Overwhelmingly, the available reforms focus on the student in the classroom and the educational system. They are about efficiency and style of learning, in the classroom. But these reforms rarely if ever are focused on how the student is going to succeed as an adult. Will students really use enquiry learning to intervene in their lives? Isn't the most effective model going to be the one that moves the classroom towards congruency with the life the student leads beyond school; the life he leads as a functioning member of a community?

EXPEDITIONARY LEARNING

Perhaps the quickest, most effective way to change the classroom is to view education as a voyage or an expedition. Expeditions have several characteristics in common. The direction is known but the terrain, obstacles, and precise goals are uncertain. Expeditions require the use of a variety of skills, some of which can be learned quickly when a problem arises, and some of which must be practiced and memorized in order to embark on or to continue the journey. Often not everybody follows precisely the same paths; some groups and individuals split off to scout alternative routes and areas. Expeditions are team efforts, but their success depends on the actions and initiative of individuals taking leadership in different ways. On an expedition, actions and inactions have real consequences.

Expeditions generally start with a mandate to explore the territory beyond a known boundary, to note any outstanding features, and to make judgments as to the potential utility and value of what is discovered. Generally, in order to be successful, expeditions make use of local knowledge.

As an aside, this description of expeditionary learning describes education as being akin to a field trip. Isn't that a perfect description of life after high school: an extended field trip?

The idea of learning and education as an expedition has been developed and implemented by Expeditionary Learning Outward Bound.[20] From the student perspective, expeditionary learning is marked by:

- A concrete connection to the world, inside and outside the classroom;
- Increased responsibility for the route to be taken and the goals;
- A clear relevance to what is learned;
- A process that is both fun and challenging;
- A valuing of both cooperation and independence in the development and presentation of strong written, oral, or other kinds of products.

From the teacher's perspective, expeditionary learning is marked by:

- Expanded time and space to make room for in-depth exploration and fieldwork using a rich variety of resources;
- Unforced integration and coordination between disciplines;
- Increased motivation, performance, and independence of students;
- A focus on issues of the attributes of character and personal growth of students as well as academic growth.

Learning expeditions can take place at any grade level, can be as inclusive or as free-standing as appropriate, and may be based on any part of the curriculum. What follows are brief descriptions of programs that have worked. In each case, the program has been included because students have had to "grow" attributes of their character in at least two or more ways. At the very minimum they have been challenged vis-à-vis their principles, and they must extend their empathy by working with folks unlike themselves. In all of the examples, students had to take risks to lead and follow others. And, in every case, students gained self-confidence and self-awareness. While most of the examples may not build all the attributes of character, they all certainly build on many of them.

EXPEDITIONARY PROJECTS

The first example is a senior project designed by each student during the spring of their junior year with one or more faculty mentors. Each project has a primary mentor and, perhaps, one or more secondary mentors who serve more or less as a dissertation committee. With the mentor, the student designs a project based on their passions or interests and develops a proposal during April for approval by a faculty committee in May. While not required, many students do fieldwork over the summer on their project. During the fall, students have a three-hour block of time, four days a week to work on their project. Every project has an English component in the form of a daily journal. A majority of projects include a historic development component, and, perhaps, a science, technology, or even foreign language component—all of which keep the registrars happy.

By Thanksgiving break, students must submit a written report on their project. During December, students make a presentation on their project to an audience of students, teachers, parents, and other individuals from outside of the school. Students received a grade based on a daily journal submitted weekly to the English faculty, their final report submitted to a faculty committee, and their presentation.

While not every student takes a risk, the majority of students extend themselves intellectually and in terms of empathy and ethics in the sense that most projects require students to be outside of the "safe" confines of the school interacting with the broader community. There is a strong expectation that students are to lead. In that sense, these projects are truly expeditions; no one is sure what the end point is going to look like.

The second project involves the production of a series of books documenting the development of Seattle and its role in the world. Two groups of students are involved: sixth graders and high school juniors. To start the project, the teacher gives the sixth graders some general background information about the book's focus. The teacher identifies individuals in and around the city willing to be interviewed by students. The students, in teams of four, develop questions and guidelines for the interviews. The interviews generally last ninety minutes, are taped, and transcribed. By consensus, the student teams decide what parts of the interview will be included in the book. Students are guided by faculty but students have the final say; the students drive the contents of the finished work. Once the content has been selected, volunteers from the community assist the students in putting the final text into publishable form.

While all of this is going on at the sixth grade, the older students are writing "sidebars" that place each interview into a social, historic, and political context. The end result of the project is a published book that explores new ground and is sold in bookstores throughout the city. The end result of the process is an extraordinary connection between students of different ages, a broad range of community members, and the people of the city, many of whom read the book.

In both projects, students' principles, empathy, and ethics are challenged by their interactions with the community. Throughout the process, everyone involved is traveling through unmapped territory and towards an uncertain outcome. Leadership and service are inherently part of the student's experience putting the projects into final form. Not everyone is following the same path, and the meaning of the journey is not always clear until it is over. These projects dissolve the boundaries between school and community and connect the students to time and place.

EXPEDITIONARY COURSES

An example of a successful expeditionary course is a summer geometry course. The students were, for the most part, highly motivated. They were at the poverty and near-poverty level, minority, rising freshman females with no background in geometry. Using a commercially available sketchpad program, the teacher set out to have the students discover triangles and the theorems that control their structure.

The teacher set the boundaries of what was known by discussing parallel lines and opposite angles. Each student was then given a cardboard triangle to observe and ask questions about. The questions were addressed and explored using the sketchpad program. Then the students discussed their questions and observations with the rest of the class. Out of this discussion more questions arose. Students could team with other students or they could work alone on answering any question. Through this process students worked their way through the geometry of triangles, other polygons, and through much of plane geometry in a period of several weeks.

It is highly likely that the teacher, by illustrating lectures using the sketchpad, could have proceeded more quickly through the material. In part, he could have been faster because he would have been more linear (no pun intended) in his approach. Had he done so, it is unlikely that the students would have been talking geometry during lunch or on the bus ride home. However, the course demanded students explore, collaborate, and negotiate their efforts. This was a wholly new process for the students, and they learned as much about this as they did about geometry.

The second example of an expeditionary course involves a summer internship for high school juniors. The students, for the most part minority, were placed with a mentor in either a corporate, university, or research facility for a period of about six weeks. The mentors were all volunteer professionals, but each had the blessings of their employers. Students were on site four days a week for between twenty and thirty hours. Every Friday, all the students met at school for a full day of seminars, classes, and reflection on their experiences. Students selected the type of setting they wished to be in and in many cases could be quite specific in the kinds of things they wanted to do. Each mentor and student had an introductory meeting and could decide on that basis whether or not to proceed. The net result of the program was a breakdown of naturally occurring barriers between corporate and town communities, between professionals and teenagers, and between schools and the marketplace.

What sets this program apart from the majority of internship programs is the fact that students returned to school every Friday. Fridays allowed the students to share their experiences, excitement, and frustrations. By talking to each other, they explored common themes and ideas of what it meant to be a professional, showing up each day in a workplace that was not of their own design and did not always work the way they would have wished. There was virtually no part of their character that came through this experience unchallenged and unchanged.

EXPEDITIONARY CURRICULA

To have an entire school or curriculum designed on the basis of expeditionary learning is neither easy nor common. They exist but I do not have personal experience with any that are successful. The only one I have personal experience with had a 6–12 curriculum centered on and integrated through the development of culture from prehistory to the present. The school was not a failure, but the curriculum was, because a coherent explanation or rationale for full implementation of the curriculum was never agreed to by the faculty.

However, expeditionary curricula do work. Examples may be found on the Web at National Environmental Education and Training Foundation (NEETF)[21] and Expeditionary Learning Outward Bound[22] or simply search the Web for "expeditionary learning." There is no need to repeat the information presented on these sites. However, to summarize:

- The schools involved are most often middle schools, with a fully integrated curriculum; 9–12 programs are becoming more common.
- In the NEETF program the integration is on the basis of environmental science. The Outward Bound Schools are less uniform in terms of their integration.
- The NEETF information does not use the phrase "expeditionary learning," but the overlap is large.
- The NEETF curricula are not focused on character development, which comes along as an afterthought, but the Outward Bound curricula are more explicitly focused on such development.
- The documented changes in student performance across the curriculum are impressive and sometimes spectacular.

Each of these efforts, whether they are a project, course, or curriculum, has the characteristics of expeditionary learning. Each of them removes the teacher from the center point of the process. In each, students assume leadership roles and responsibility for what happens. In each, the end point is not clear at the start, and not all students travel the same path, but through sharing and interaction, all of the students end up at the same spot. And it is not a bad spot. It's a spot achieved through the exercise and development of character. Academically, students very likely have achieved no less than they would have under another approach. More likely, they have achieved more.

Achievement is what a classroom should be all about. But improved achievement is not just about more and more, in less and less time. It is about taking the time to help students learn how to learn and how to think. And it is about ensuring every student the opportunity to succeed. High expectations must be tempered by a willingness to reach out to every student using whatever legitimate means are available. Expeditionary learning allows individualization without stigma and without loss of content or rigor.

SUMMARY OF EXPEDITIONARY LEARNING

Expeditionary learning has dramatic impacts on the individual student, and restructures the classroom in fundamental ways. If this approach were to become pervasive within a school, there would be some important changes in the structure and function of the school.

First, with this approach schools would become more inclusive. Inclusion is certainly about race, ethnicity, socioeconomic status, and gender. But it is about much more. It is about recognizing excellence wherever, whenever, and however it is found. All schools talk about test scores and college acceptances. Some also talk about athletic success. Fewer still talk about the arts. Virtually no school boasts about the beauty and excellence found in those daily decisions that students can make when the teacher is not the sole directional beacon. With expeditionary learning, students have the opportunity to demonstrate excellence in a myriad of ways following their own paths to a common academic excellence.

Second, expeditionary learning creates a less autocratic social structure more in keeping with both the culture and social structures familiar to the student. The traditional classroom structure, with the all-powerful teacher up front and the students dutifully sitting in rows receiving wisdom, is a concept that goes against the grain of much the students see in the wider culture. With expeditionary learning, the social dynamic is more fluid. Both students and teacher move in and out of positions of leadership and responsibility quickly and easily.

Third, with expeditionary learning, schools are far more likely to be places of joy. Joy is what a runner feels when exhausting workouts and self-discipline lead to a personal best, and, perhaps, to victory. Students are willing learners. They are built to learn and, no matter what we do to them, they will learn. And every time they do, they beat their previous personal best. That should cause joy and celebration, and it almost always does, away from school. Too often at school, it is seen solely as a rung on a ladder of soul-crushing tedium: the bottom is lost and the top seems impossibly distant. With expeditionary learning, every new discovery can be joyfully celebrated in the here and now as having an intrinsic value for the student. If this happens, the endless journey will take care of itself.

There is no single recipe for successful teaching; expeditionary learning is no exception. Of all the major reforms presently out there, it may be the most effective. Many of the other reforms will not be as effective to the extent that they consider either teachers or students passive and indistinguishable, one from another. They will fail to capitalize on the power of variety that already exists in any and all classrooms. Worse, to the extent that the reform is modeled on an instructivist, top-down, one-size-fits-all mode of operation, it will fatally poison the creative, inventive process that is American education at its best. Does anybody seriously believe that, in and of itself, the NCLB approach will make us competitive with China, South Korea, or India? The NCLB cannot and will not generate well-trained, creative engineers, scientists, thinkers, or doers.

SYSTEMS THINKING AND EXPEDITIONARY LEARNING

There is another reason that expeditionary learning works where other reforms may not be as effective. The expeditionary approach is congruent with systems thinking. A list of congruencies would include at least the following, in no particular order:

- Both are constructivist in nature. It may be possible, but I would imagine difficult, for a teacher to be entirely instructivist using systems thinking and models. But the power of the approach comes from students using systems thinking to build their own models. Expeditionary learning is inherently constructivist; a teacher-lead, instructivist expedition is an oxymoron.
- Both approaches address the complexity that is a classroom. Both allow students to travel different routes to the end point. There is no necessary assumption of student sameness either in interest, learning styles, or background.
- Used appropriately, both approaches move the classroom from a teacher-centric or text-centric condition to a student-centric condition.
- Both are inherently interdisciplinary. They go where the path leads without regard for disciplinary boundaries. This often means the inherent logic of the trip or the model demands crossing boundaries.
- Both start with the known and the secure and move quickly into the unknown and unique. This means that a larger percentage of the student's education is a case of authentically learning the unknown.
- Both are effective vehicles for learning content while simultaneously teaching skills useful in the adult world.
- To be successful in either, the student has to keep his eye on both the deductive and inductive process. The mapping a route to the goal and understanding the meaning and implications of the discoveries en route are equally important.
- Systems thinking, model building, and expeditionary learning are all inherently creative enterprises.
- Both systems provide a solid basis for increasing the student's historicity by showing him how to identify effective leverage points for changing the status quo. Systems thinking helps in the identification, and expeditionary learning gives him practice in acting to bring about change.

- Woven together, they can produce a seamless whole usable across age groups and disciplines.
- Neither approach is exclusive. Both can be used to a greater or lesser degree in conjunction with any other constructivist approach to teaching. It is not an all-or-nothing situation.
- And, finally, systems thinking, model building, and expeditionary learning are fun. Students may work harder than they have before and may have to become more personally invested than before, but they do have a very good time.

NOTES

1. R. Stephens and E. V. Scott, "Ensuring Workforce Skills of the Future: The Birth to Work Pipeline," 2003, p. 4, retrieved January 15, 2008, from http://www.cpec.ca.gov/completereports/externaldocuments/birth_to _work_pipelinev50.pdf.

2. R. Louv, *Last Child in the Woods; Saving Our Children from Nature-Deficit Disorder* (Chapel Hill, NC: Algonquin Books, 2005).

3. M. McLuhan, "Cybernation and Culture," pp. 105 in *The Social Impact of Cybernetics*, ed. C. R. Dechert (New York: Simon & Schuster, 1966).

4. Definition from *The Free Dictionary*. Retrieved September 26, 2007, from http://www.thefreedictionary.com/phantasmagoria.

5. R. S. Wurman, *Information Anxiety 2*, p. 40 (Indianapolis: Que, 2001).

6. B. Richmond, "Systems Thinking and the STELLA Software," p. 2. Retrieved January 20, 2008, from http://www.iseesystems.com/resources/ Articles/STELLA%20IST%20-%20Chapter%201.pdf.

7. Waters Foundation, "Related Best Practice." Retrieved January 20, 2008, from http://www.watersfoundation.org/index.cfm?fuseaction=stdm .relatedbestPractice

8. M. F. Scheier and C. S. Carver, "On the Power of Positive Thinking: The Benefits of Being Optimistic," *Current Directions in Psychological Science* 2, no. 1 (1993): 26–30.

9. Scheier and Carver, "On the Power of Positive Thinking," 26–30.

10. M. Jacobson and Working Group 2 Collaborators, "Complex Systems And Education: Cognitive Learning And Pedagogical Perspectives" (section 2, with internal references deleted). Retrieved February 22, 2008, from http://www.necsi.org/events/cxedk16/cxedk16_2.html.

11. See http://secondlife.com/.

12. G. Kearsley, "Mental Models," sec. 3.8, in *Explorations in Learning & Instruction: The Theory into Practice Database*. Retrieved February 12, 2008, from http://tip.psychology.org/models.html.

13. B. R. Gaines and M. L. G. Shaw, "Personal Construct Psychology and the Cognitive Revolution." Retrieved February 12, 2008, from http://pages.cpsc.ucalgary.ca/~gaines/reports/PSYCH/SIM/index.html.

14. These diagrams are drawn with the MapSys program retrieved January 12, 2008, from http://simtegra.com/system-dynamics-modeling-software.html.

15. There are two software packages commonly used to build and run simulation models: Vensim from http://www.vensim.com/software.html or Stella from http://www.iseesystems.com/.

16. J. Forrester, "Road Maps: A Guide to Learning System Dynamics," 1994. Retrieved February 14, 2008, from http://web.mit.edu/sysdyn/road-maps/toc.html or http://sysdyn.clexchange.org/road-maps/rm-toc.html.

17. J. West, K. Denton, and E. M. Reaney, "The Kindergarten Year," 2001. Retrieved February 14, 2008, from http://nces.ed.gov/pubs2001/2001023.pdf.

18. J. S. Renzulli, "The Definition of High-End Learning." Retrieved January 20, 2008, from http://www.gifted.uconn.edu/sem/semart10.html.

19. D. Brin, "Science & Civilization March On! (Non-political)," February 23, 2008, [Comment 1] Contrary Brin. Retrieved February 23, 2008, from http://davidbrin.blogspot.com/2008/02/science-civilization-march-on-non.html.

20. Expeditionary Learning Schools: Outward Bound. Retrieved February 14, 2008, from http://www.elob.org/.

21. The National Environmental Education & Training Foundation, "Environment-Based Education: Creating High-Performance Schools and Students," 2000. Retrieved March 1, 2008, from http://www.neefusa.org/pdf/NEETF8400.pdf.

22. See our results. Retrieved March 1, 2008, from Expeditionary Learning Schools Outward Bound Web site: http://www.elschools.org/results/index.html.

CHAPTER 4

Managing the Classroom

READING STUDENTS

It is a true statement that no matter how wonderful the teacher is, no matter how compelling the class content, no matter what, there will be the student who comes to class disconnected, uninterested, or unwilling to be there. No teachers are immune; it can happen to any class.

Part of the art of teaching is to be able to read the students as they come through the door. Most of the time, students make it pretty clear how and what they feel within seconds of walking in the door. However, it does not take much to imagine a school where that would not be the case for cultural, social, or psychological reasons.

I was once at such a school, and I found it very hard to read most of the students quickly. To make our lives easier, I built a eudemony meter for the classroom. Eudemony is a measure of general well-being. A list of factors reducing eudemony would include, but not be limited to, stress, insecurity, conflict, general malaise, and exhaustion. The meter consisted of an open pine cabinet with a layer of cork in the back with a seven-inch circle inscribed. At the base of the cabinet were five containers of push pins; green, blue, clear, yellow, and red.

The cabinet was situated so I could not see the color pin the student put into the cork on entering the class. Before I started class, I would look at the pattern in the target and knew immediately what I was dealing with. Some days I could go for broke and some days I couldn't. Some days, I just abandoned the lesson plan, and did something else entirely because it was really green or really red.

There are a lot of ways that such a system could be abused. Students could intentionally mislead either alone or in concert. Since I did not count the pins, they might put in an extra red or two. They might change the pins already in the target. They might not play at all. In all the time I used the meter, about seven years, it was never messed with. In those instances where I had a single red at the start of class for two or three days running, the students always made sure I knew who was having a bad time. They never did it outright; it was always in code, but they made sure I knew. The student in question was always grateful.

The only time I had trouble with it was when, after I had used for about four years, I figured I knew the student culture and the students well enough to get rid of it. So I moved it to the back of the room and was faced with open rebellion. The students simply refused to start class until it was returned to its rightful place. They claimed that it was the first and only time anybody had asked. I do not believe that it really was the first time, but it may have been the first time they were aware of being asked.

When faced with the disconnected student, the teacher has a couple of alternatives, all of which can be equally correct or equally wrong depending on the particular circumstances. A possible response is to simply ignore the student's presence. In some situations this is clearly the best alternative. However, in almost all circumstances, especially if it rarely occurs for a particular student, it would probably be a better option to ask what is going on. Students really appreciate being asked. Often they do not feel anybody is asking or listening. They are happy simply to have some adult listen. Asking the question, really hearing the answer, and responding appropriately is a measure of the master teacher.

CLASSROOM MANAGEMENT

Having the ability to read the students as they come through the door is only the first step. The second, far more difficult, step is to effectively respond to what you've learned. Whatever you do is called classroom management.

As the phrase is usually used, "classroom management" is all about discipline. More than anything else, it is classroom management that terrifies soon-to-be teachers. It consumes a great deal of psychic energy; witness that if you search the Internet for the phrase, you will get about 3.5 million hits. Not all those hits are really about maintaining order in the classroom, but even if only a tenth of them are about teaching, those 350,000 hits are an indication of where it ranks with teachers.

There are a number of different, named approaches to maintaining order in the classroom. A common approach is called "Assertive Discipline," developed in 1976 by Lee Canter.[1] Although it has been modified in the last thirty years to a more open and democratic approach than Canter proposed, the core of Assertive Discipline is based on the establishment of explicit classroom rules by the teacher, for the teacher. If the students break the rules, the teacher must consistently increase sanctions with each infraction. Although Canter writes about rewarding students for behaving well, there is less discussion of that aspect in the writings of others.

Many teachers do not stick with Assertive Discipline for very long. The approach has tremendous appeal for beginning teachers; it gives them a sense of control and empowerment in the face of what they fear will be chaos. However, as teachers become more confident in their abilities, they tend to modify the approach beyond recognition.

Assertive Discipline is a first cousin of McGregor's Theory X that workers, read students, are inherently unmotivated, lazy, uninterested, must be threatened with punishment to work, shirk responsibility, and want the security of rules above all else. In addition, the only rewards that motivate workers are extrinsic to the job, that is, paychecks. Very few teachers view their students through the lens of Theory X. Instead, congruent with their optimism, their compassion, their trust in students, and the goal of increasing student historicity, teachers tend view their students through the lens of Theory Y.

Theory Y is essentially the polar opposite of Theory X. Theory Y teachers believe that students will get as much satisfaction and reward inside the classroom from doing the best they know when faced with appropriate levels of challenge as they do outside the classroom. Achievement will rise if students are given the freedom to do their best, if they are given the needed support, encouraged to use their ingenuity, and given the responsibility to get the job done.

Theory X is about rules, constraints, and punishments. Theory Y is about shared goals, creativity, and freedom. The two theories are the two extremes of a continuum. On any given day at any given moment, teachers may be exhibit behavior from one side or the other of the center point, but most master teachers find themselves spending far more time closer to the Y end rather than the X end. That is as it should be, because students working in a Theory X classroom will not, indeed cannot, develop the kinds of social capital or worldview needed to support an effective degree of historicity.

CLASSROOM MANAGEMENT: REQUISITE VARIETY

Sure, every classroom needs rules. The students probably should not be dancing on the desks. The question is, how many and what kind? The starting point for the development of classroom management has to be the classroom goals. If the primary goal is to keep students safe, both psychologically and physically, then there has to be a certain number of inviolate rules to that end. Those rules have to be explicit, but no master teacher is going to be caught in a box of having limited, explicit sanctions imposed for every infraction.

There are at least three sources of inappropriate behavior in the classroom. The first is exuberance and good humor. The students simply want to see if they can fly. The second is that the students are thrashing around in the deep end of the pool with no idea of how to swim. The third source is a paucity of human spirit leading to willful destruction, bullying, and malfeasance. It is clear that imposing identical sanctions for these different kinds of intention will be counterproductive and actually destructive in terms of other classroom goals. Do we really want to sanction a bully in the same way we sanction a joyful experimentation? Do we really want to treat joyful experimentation in the same way we treat a drowning student?

Is this injustice? Perhaps, and certainly intention is not always as clear and pure as it might be. But the students generally have a fairly clear, realistic, and nuanced picture of their peers; they are likely to accept different sanctions for similar acts as long as their perception of intention is similar to the teacher's; after all, that is pretty much the way the world works. Intention does count for something.

So once again we are back to the question of what counts in the classroom. Do we ignore the complexity of the system and treat every student as a cog on the wheel? If so, then classroom management devolves to operant conditioning with rules and rewards. If not, then any approach to classroom management must address the law of requisite variety where "regulation is then possible only if the regulating system is as various and flexible (responsive to changes) as the system to be regulated."[2] In other words, the teacher, as regulator, must be able to recognize and respond to the broad range or variety of inputs represented by the students on any given day.

There is not a chance in the world that any teacher can match the variety represented by a class of twenty students. To take a trivial example, if students vary on only one trait that can be "off" or "on," the class can achieve significantly more than a million states. So, if perfection is impossible, how much variety is enough?

That is probably the wrong question; enough is never going to be enough. The better question is how do you maximize the variety you can respond to effectively? The short answer includes:

- Maximize your competence, compassion, and life experience;
- Keep your eye on the goal of increasing the student's historicity;

- Trust that the students are doing the very best they know how;
- Maximize your ability to laugh at yourself and the situation;
- Leave your ego at the classroom door;
- And, understand the difference between discipline and punishment.

CLASSROOM MANAGEMENT: FIRST RULE

For competent, compassionate master teachers, classroom management starts way before the first student comes in the door. The foundation of effective management is having a classroom, both physically and psychologically, where students want to be.

Obviously teachers cannot control the number of windows or the physical layout of the classroom. But they can sometimes agitate successfully for the color on the walls, and they can certainly control what's on the walls. Some of the homiest rooms I've ever seen looked like a packrat's dream, with student work selected over the years hung from every spot available. In another class, with large windows in the back, the class created and painted a totemic design representing who they wanted to be on the glass. Certainly all those department stores cannot be wrong; ambient music can set the tone and color the experience of a space.

What can be accomplished is dependent on the culture of the school, whether the space is shared with other teachers, the resources available, and the space itself. In no case can the teacher abdicate responsibility for the condition of the room, so all the changes and improvements are negotiated with a goal to increase student ownership of the space.

But no matter how homey the classroom is, the students will not feel ownership of the space unless they also feel safe, physically and psychologically. A necessary basis for students feeling safe is the presence of rules that are held inviolate. The rule that leaps to mind is the golden rule, "Do unto others . . ." The trouble is that this rule is meaningless to precisely those students who have the greatest tendency to create social havoc. They are bullies who have "already been done to" and see the world as being a place where you do first before it can be done to you. A better rule might be, "You can say, or do, anything provided it is true, kind, and useful (it gets us down the road to where we want to be)."

This rule has several advantages over the more common golden rule. The first is that it provides a launching pad for helping a student learn one of the really tough lessons in this world: my opinion on something is not automatically the truth about something. Different worldviews can see the same evidence supporting different opinions. Students often find this difficult to accept without resorting to an ad hominem argument such as, "He's just dumb," which is probably not true, not kind, and doesn't get us farther down the road to understanding. The first part of this rule legitimizes discussions of, but is not limited to, what is truth, how do we know it, what is the difference between evidence and proof?

The second part of the rule concerning kindness legitimizes discussions of ethics, the nature of the other, and interactive reciprocity. Beyond that, it absolutely legitimizes discussions of manners in particular and politeness in general. Many students do not understand the need to switch codes in different situations and do not know the appropriate codes. This part of the rule allows all of that to be discussed.

The third part of the rule, about getting farther down the road, needs to be understood broadly. Getting farther down the road is not just about the curricular tasks of the classroom. It is also about social cohesion, individual development, exploration, and the development of the attributes of character. If the class forms a task-only group, it will tend to be brittle and break apart in the face of difficulty or perturbation. A certain amount of getting down the road is about group structure and dynamics; most often, it's about fun. This rule about truth, kindness, and efficacy can be the basis for a safe class for every student. More important, the rule provides a foundation for giving the students skills and understandings that will serve them well, very well, in the world outside of school.

CLASSROOM MANAGEMENT: ESSENTIAL QUESTIONS

Master teachers set a foundation for classroom management before the first student comes through the door by the curricular decisions they make. Students are less likely to need draconian management if they are feeling successful. There may be, of course, a very thin boundary between a student succeeding and a student feeling bored. Boredom is the kiss of death, so the trick is to develop a curriculum that allows for success for all without being stultifying for the majority of students.

The definition of master teachers includes competence, compassion, and life experience. The dimension of competence means that the teachers have a deep and broad understanding of the subject taught. They have the confidence of knowing that while they cannot answer every question, they can always get to where they want to go. More importantly, they have a clear idea of what essential questions lie at the core of the subject taught and what enduring understandings the students should have long after the students have forgotten the teacher's name.

But knowing the essential questions is not enough. The essential questions in many disciplines are likely to be the same for a Ph.D. candidate and a high school senior, but the expression of both the questions and the answers is likely to be very different. A master teacher has the compassion, and the ability to meet the students where they are, to formulate the questions and the answers in ways that make sense to their students. Further, the combination of competence and compassion allows the teacher to formulate the questions and understandings and to choose any one of the myriad approaches possible. Every essential question can be attacked in multiple ways; the decision has to be which way makes the most sense and is most appropriate, interesting, and effective for the students.

The life experience of the master teacher allows the teacher to connect the essential questions and enduring understandings to the world. It is not enough that the questions and understandings connect to where the students are at the moment. They have to connect to where the students think they are going. The students must be convinced that the questions make a difference now and tomorrow. If the teacher's life experience does not support making these kinds of connections, he or she might seriously consider why this material is being taught.

The resultant curriculum will have the following characteristics:

- It will be relevant; it will be important in the here and now and in the future.
- It will be interesting; it will apply to the students themselves and their existence.
- It will be integrated; it will be connected to other parts of the curriculum and students' lives.
- It will be congruent; it will be closely linked to and build on what went before.
- It will be short; it will be presented in coherent units with an end point.

Some of these characteristics, especially coherence and end point, seem to be diametrically opposed to the suggestions made earlier vis-à-vis expeditionary learning and the systems classroom. However, there is an important distinction here. What we are talking about here are those parts of the curriculum delivered, in whatever fashion, lecture, worksheets, and so on, by the teacher. The other parts of the curriculum, expeditions lead by the students, are probably less coherent and probably should not have a clear, unambiguous end point.

CLASSROOM MANAGEMENT: CLASSROOM CULTURE

So classroom management is not just about rules. Classroom management is about connectedness between student and teacher. It is about space and content creating an ambience that meets student and teacher needs and wants. In short, it is about the classroom culture.

Saying that it is about culture has some important implications. The first is that culture is a complex interaction of multiple elements, each of which has both substantive nature and a shared, context-specific symbolic meaning that may or may not have a tight connection to the substantive nature of the element itself. This means all culture is homegrown; not just for a particular class, but a particular class each year. The teacher is a major factor in the establishment of the culture. But the other elements, notably the experiences, meanings, and worldviews of the students, are going to have an impact on the formation of a culture.

Further, while all involved may have rough agreement on the culture desired, the culture itself is autopoietic or self-generating. Autopoiesis is the ability of a system to produce, maintain, and change itself using its structure and self-contained interactions. The autopoietic system is not built according to a plan imposed from beyond its boundaries. It is self-generating in the same sense that an organism is self-generating.

Autopoietic culture is not random, but is very unpredictable. Very minor, unmeasured, and unknown differences in inputs can produce qualitatively different outcomes, each of which must be assigned significant probabilities of occurrence. Autopoietic structures can be shaped by controlling some of the inputs in the same sense that organisms can be shaped by controlling diet, health, or experience. But the manipulation of inputs does not guarantee the desired output; think of children with similar inputs, such as fraternal twins, and the possible variations in outcomes. Unless the teacher can control every single input, a manifest impossibility, the teacher cannot control, in detail, the formation of the classroom culture.

Like an organism, a classroom culture has a life cycle involving at least three stages: immaturity, maturity, and senescence. Immaturity is characterized by energy investment in growth with increasing complexity, and plasticity in structure or behavior. This is what happens in September when both teacher and students are investing energy in making connections with each other, the subject, and the space itself. Everybody is busy establishing social and physical territories, personas, and expectations. This is the stage when the culture can be most easily shaped and the teacher takes an active role in doing so.

Maturity is characterized by moderate growth in complexity, a low expenditure of energy on maintenance with reduced plasticity, and a high expenditure of energy in "doing." This is the class everyone dreams of, on task, comfortable, and stable. Most cultures spend the greater part of the time at this stage.

Senescence is characterized by a low expenditure of energy on "doing," a high expenditure on maintenance, a high ratio of inputs to outputs, and a reduced plasticity of structure or function except for breakdowns. This is the class in June.

All classroom cultures go through this cycle during the course of a year but a truncated version of the cycle occurs during every forty-five- to fifty-minute class. The cycle is not just about age or time. The cycle can be interrupted; the loss of a teacher will always put the class back to immaturity.

Master teachers can get the class through immaturity quickly and can delay senescence, but the cycle will not be denied; it happens.

CLASSROOM MANAGEMENT: THE DESIRED CULTURE

The idea that the class culture is autopoietic does not mean that the teacher is helpless in the face of a counterproductive culture. The first question must be how does the teacher evaluate the culture? Is there a criterion that allows one culture to be judged as better or worse?

The most obvious criterion has to be, does the culture enhance or detract from the student's degree of historicity? If we assume for the moment that the student is a psychologically healthy individual with a least a modicum of self-worth, the student's quality of life will be enhanced if the three elements of historicity—worldview, social capital, and knowledge and skills—are more or less congruent.

If one of the elements of historicity is not sufficient to support one or both of the others, the student's quality of life will suffer. If the worldview supports or demands an intervention on his part, but he does not have the social capital to support the intervention, the student will feel frustrated. If the student has, or is learning, the knowledge and skills to support an intervention that his worldview suggests is useless, meaningless, or damaging, he will be at least bored and possibly rebellious. If his store of fiscal or social capital is insufficient to support his knowledge and skills in a way congruent with his worldview, he may become a Machiavellian manipulator of the social context.

None of these outcomes is beneficial for either the student or the class. Therefore, the culture to be desired is the one that allows the student maximum freedom to improve the congruency of the three components. So what does such a culture look like? That is a difficult question to answer in detail, but such a culture will have most, if not all of the following characteristics:

- It will not be text- or teacher-centric. Both tend to treat students as indistinguishable ciphers without idiosyncrasies.
- It will be about direction rather than prescription because that allows multiple paths for students to follow on their expeditionary journeys through the material.
- It will create multiple approaches vis-à-vis the content of the curriculum and will celebrate multiple demonstrations of excellence and achievement.
- The question will always be more valued than the answer.
- The assumption will always be that the students are doing the best they know how, if not in class, in living their life.
- A corollary of the above statement is that no insult will be taken if none is intended.

I recognize that this sounds like a warm, fuzzy, vacuous cliché where the individual is celebrated, everybody is committed to traveling in the same direction, and all students are well above the class average. However, this sort of culture is rarely achieved in most classes, even when the explicit goal is to create such. In part, the difficulty is in inputs that the teacher does not control: administrative, curricular, parental, and cultural demands imposed from outside the class. But the lethal difficulty often arrives with the students themselves. If the student does not find utility in the class or if he does not believe that the class helps him fulfill his aspirations, present or future, he will not be committed to travel down the road with the class. It is not that he marches to a different drummer; he may not march at all. If he does not march at all, that, perforce, will reverberate through the class culture and change it to something less than wonderful.

CLASSROOM MANAGEMENT: CULTURE AND BEHAVIOR

The classroom culture is shaped by the students and shapes the students' behavior in broadly predictable ways. Technically, student behavior may be chaotic but is not random. The behavior exhibited is the result of the interactions between of several variables: the present rate of fulfillment, in terms of a student aspiration or goal; the reward, or predicted change in fulfillment resulting from some action undertaken at a reasonable cost; in a classroom that the student values to some degree, or not.[3]

If the student's level of aspiration is greater than the present rate of fulfillment, but that rate may be increased by a reasonable action within a valued class, the primary response is to comply with the classroom norms and work to achieve class objectives because doing so supports achievement of the student's goals. A second possible response is to beat the system, achieving sanctioned rewards through unsanctioned means, unsanctioned rewards through sanctioned means, or unsanctioned rewards through unsanctioned means, and, with luck, not getting caught.

If the student's aspiration is greater than the present rate of fulfillment, but the rate of fulfillment is equal to or greater than any increase expected from a reasonable action within a valued class, the student may search for a source of fulfillment outside of the class. If successful, the student will leave or attempt escape. If unsuccessful, the student may try to alter the class culture to make the reward attainable. The alteration may be "deviant," disruptive behavior that breaks cultural norms, defensive behavior denying or rationalizing the status quo, or regressive behavior.

If the student's aspiration is less than the present rate of fulfillment, but the present rate is as low as can be, and the class is not positively valued, the student will carry out avoidance and defensive behaviors similar to the above paragraph, with the primary difference being that the source is over-satiation rather than under-satiation.

If the student's aspirations are being more or less met, and the present rate would be increased by any reasonable action within a positively valued class, the student will behave in a way to maintain the status quo with a minimum of invested effort.

If the present rate of fulfillment is equal or greater than the student's aspirations, and unchanged by any reasonable action in any valuation of the class, the student is getting more than he wants without an expenditure of energy; he is likely to withdraw psychologically or physically to another place.

Although the teacher might predict the broad outlines of the student's behavior by understanding the interactions of his goals, rate of goal fulfillment, and his assessment of the utility or value of the class, the details of what he will do are set by the contents of his historicity. His goals are, in a sense, his worldview made operational. The action he takes to achieve a reward is a function of his technical knowledge and skills. The cost he can afford to expend is often a function of his social capital. These aspects are to some degree idiosyncratic and difficult to predict. In addition, student goals are neither quantitatively nor qualitatively stable. They may change minute-to-minute and certainly vary day-to-day.

Prediction with anything other than very broad brushstrokes is impossible. The real value here is that we now have some particular questions to ask about any classroom culture including, but certainly not limited to:

• Which (whose) goals does the culture address, in what ways, and with what effect?
• To what extent is the student an active participant in determining fulfillment rates?
• What sorts of actions are supported by the culture, and can students afford them?
• Is the culture such that students value it or see a utility coming from it?

CLASSROOM CULTURE: SEEDING THE CULTURE

If the classroom culture is organic, autopoietic, and complex, how is it that master teachers seem to get it right, time after time, often in the face of highly variable students? The short answer is goodwill.

Every year, most students come into class for the first time hoping that this is going to be the class or the teacher that lights their fire, keeps them on the edge of their chairs, and keeps them excited, successful, proud, and joyous. If indeed they are walking into a classroom of a master teacher, that teacher may already have a reputation for doing at least some of this, which gives them even more hope.

It is this hope that allows students to be open to the unknown and willing to take, perhaps, a certain risk by going along with the program for a while. It is this honeymoon period, even though short, that allows master teachers to get it right more often than not. When I started teaching, I was told not to smile until Thanksgiving. It was a joke but many a truth is said in jest. The idea was that the student had to know who was in charge, who called the shots, and who should not be messed with. Did it work? I guess so. Was it fun? No, and I would not recommend that tactic to anybody.

The master teacher has the competence, compassion, and life experience to effectively shape the outlines of the class culture during those initial weeks of class. When the students come into class for the first time, the master teacher has a curricular structure in place. The contents may or may not be a review, but in every case provides a context for what is to come and why it is important. The master teacher has the life experience and compassion to tie this content directly to the students' lives. Figuratively, why should they being doing this? What value will it have today, tomorrow, and the day after? The most important point here is that the reason for making this effort is not because the teacher says it is important and certainly not just so the students can get to the next step.

The content of the course must have inherent value that students understand in terms of their worldview. One of the requirements of any culture is that participants have at least overlapping worldviews. In most classes, the worldviews the students bring through the door already overlap in very significant ways. In order to shape the class culture, it behooves the teacher to make explicit what those overlaps are vis-à-vis the curriculum.

It may be that the teacher has to construct these shared understandings from scratch. It may be that the students have little or no idea why they are doing what they're doing. Be that as it may, this effort is worth making.

Probably, the crucial skill for this task is the ability to hear what messages the students are sending during the first days of class. It will call on the teacher's competence to pick and choose the essential questions with the greatest relevance, his life experience to tie the essential questions to the world as his students understand it, and his compassion to make all of the above meaningful to the students.

If teachers succeed in this task, they have set a firm foundation for the growth of trust between them and the students. If teachers fail this task by either "getting off to a good start" with the content or otherwise ignoring the messages sent by the students, as days pass and history accrues, trust becomes more difficult to develop. Trust is the essential ingredient of an effective class culture; without it, an effective culture may be doomed; classroom management becomes problematic at best and a nightmare at worst.

CLASSROOM CULTURE: CENTRAL VARIABLES

Nothing that I have said about classroom culture is particularly new or different from what others have said. However a remaining point worth thinking about is the question of, how do cultures spontaneously change?

A classroom culture is in every way a system and not an aggregation of autonomous bits and pieces. In theory, this means that every element is connected or interacting directly or indirectly with other elements. Centrality is a measure of this connectedness. Examples of elements that are usually highly connected include course content, shared student goals, the physical arrangement of the class, and teacher characteristics and expectations. Elements that are unlikely to be central might include style of dress, conditions at home, and time of day.

A lack of centrality is not a lack of importance to the individual student. Conditions at home may have paramount centrality for the individual student, and the teacher must respond to this fact, but conditions at home are likely to have low centrality to the class culture. With older students, style of dress may be highly central to their own image or, in the case of cliques and gangs, their social capital.

Rapid cultural change is entirely possible and even expected in those elements that are not central. It is almost a case of simple inertia. A low level of connectedness means that the element can change without dragging a mass of other elements along with it. This is the definition of minor change; an element can change without disrupting the cultural fabric. This kind of change can be triggered by small changes in inputs: a rainy day, a lost football game, a poorly designed curricular unit, or virtually any other perturbation. The wonderful thing is that once the perturbation ceases and the input returns to normal, the culture will probably, with some delay, do the same.

Highly connected elements resist change and are probably not responsive to small changes in inputs. If the perturbation is short lived and not too egregious, the students and the teacher do not actually ignore it, they absorb the change as an anomaly and move on. The culture does not change.

If the change in input is significant, lasts a long time, and affects a highly centralized element of the culture, both students and teacher will experience increasing levels of frustration. The culture is no longer functioning in a way to meet their needs. There are two responses possible to this situation. The initial reaction is to do what is being done harder, more effectively, and longer. If you are a fisherman not catching fish, the first response is to fish harder, smarter, and longer. And you do that even though you get hungry. And if fishing is central to your life, you do it even when you are really hungry because you define yourself as a fisherman. But there may come a time when you throw the whole thing over and become a farmer. This is a catastrophic change, where a catastrophe is defined as a radical change in conditions, not better, not worse, just very, very different.

The same thing may happen to a culture. A small change of input affecting a central element may be absorbed for a period of time to be followed by a rapid, significant, autopoietic restructuring.

CLASSROOM CULTURE: CRITICAL VARIABLES

Classroom cultures can spontaneously restructure themselves in the face of change inside or outside of the cultural boundaries. Sometimes the restructuring occurs easily, and sometimes not so easily. The difference depends on the centrality of the element undergoing the change. Those elements that are structurally highly connected tend to be those elements that have a critical function in the system.

A critical variable is defined as one that if it changes beyond a narrow range of values, up, down, or sometimes either, causes the system to dissolve. As a common example, consider body temperature for mammals. It the temperature varies in either direction beyond very narrow limits, the mammal ceases to function.

The critical variables for a classroom could include, but not be limited to: inputs to the classroom including materials, supplies, space, and teacher commitment or experience; endogenous elements including aggregate rates of student need fulfillment, levels of frustration and trust, commitment to common goals, and student valuation of the class; or outputs including noise, test scores, or student and parent complaints. Each of these variables can, if uncontrolled, cause the class to devolve into some other kind of system.

However, in any viable, ongoing classroom, the critical variables are not uncontrolled. They are highly connected to another set of variables, the adaptive variables. Technically, adaptive variables can be described as elements in negative feedback loops that dampen the rate and scope of change in the critical variables. Less formally, the adaptive variables are the traits that one sees and feels on entering the function classroom. If you were to describe to a friend what it was like to be in the class, how it felt, and how it worked, for the most part, you would be using the adaptive variables.

There are more than a few critical variables in each classroom, and it is unlikely that both teacher and students would agree on what they all were. But if the classroom is to remain effective and viable, there must be feedback loops associated with every one of them. Some of the feedback loops run through some combination of students, parents, administrators, or others, and are independent of the teacher. However, again if the class is to remain effective and viable, most of the loops must run through and be mediated by the teacher. That flow and processing of information is the core of the feedback loop. The response is the adaptive variable.

An example of what I mean is provided by the eudemony meter described several pages ago. The level of eudemony is determined by factors both inside and outside the classroom, and is, in most classes, going to be a centralized, critical variable affecting other aspects of the cultural system. Too low a level will raise levels of frustration, and will lower levels of effort, risk-taking, and valuation of the class. Too high a level will have less predictable results, but at a minimum might increase risk taking to possibly unacceptable levels, and possibly lower the valuation of the class; after all, since all is well with the world, who needs this? But, if the adaptive variable, be it a change in program, a change in process, a change in focus, or a change in activity is successful, the level of eudemony is ameliorated to the point where the class can commence, that day or perhaps the next.

CLASSROOM CULTURE: SCHISMOGENESIS

There is one more change process found in classroom cultures that teachers must have on their radar screens and be sensitive to. This process, schismogenesis, was first described by Gregory Bateson in his book, *Naven*, and revisited in *Steps to an Ecology of Mind*.[4] There are two forms of schismogenesis; complementary and symmetrical.

Complementary schismogenesis occurs between two groups or individuals with unequal power where one is dominant and the other submissive. Schismogenesis occurs when the more dominant becomes more dominant and the submissive becomes more submissive. In healthy cultures, there are mechanisms that short-circuit the differentiation so that it does not proceed very far. If these short-circuits do not exist or are ineffective, the situation can spiral out of control.

An example of this process is documented in the Stanford prison experiment.[5] Schismogenesis explains how, as the experiment proceeded, several of the guards became progressively more sadistic — particularly at night, when they thought the cameras were off. Experimenters said approximately one-third of the guards exhibited "genuine" sadistic tendencies.[6]

For example, suppose the students do not do their homework. The teacher might respond with a punishment of some sort. The students accept the punishment, but still do not do the homework. The teacher ups the ante; the students grudgingly accept, but still no homework. Sometimes coercion is effective; over the short term, behavior changes, but we are now in danger of an upward spiral of punishment and nonperformance, or distance and confrontation. If nothing intervenes, this is the situation generated by the "Assertive Discipline" approach spoken of earlier. The classroom culture will be shredded, and the class will devolve into armed camps. An effective short-circuit is the teacher's trust that the students are living their life the best they know how. The teacher starts asking questions about what is happening and why. The "why" questions are about causation, and the focus shifts from coercion to solution.

Student-student interactions are also subject to complementary schismogenesis. This is a process that creates bullies and victims in a range of forms from physical to psychological and social. Complementary schismogenesis may not occur any more often between students than between students and teacher, but it is like a fever in young children. Students do not have fully developed control mechanisms or short-circuits, and schismogenesis can escalate rapidly with damaging, or rarely, fatal results.

I wish I knew an easy, surefire, and simple short-circuit for bullying. I do not, and I have never met a teacher who did. It is certainly easier to stop if two conditions are met. The first is that the power structure, read, the teacher, the explicit rules, and the administration, does not tolerate it. The second condition is that the student subculture in the class contains a sense of "all for one; one for all." Together, these will preclude a lot of bullying, but not all. The most effective antidotes for bullying are compassion on the part of the teacher, and a reciprocal trust between the students and the teacher. These two cultural elements often can shortstop schismogenesis almost as soon as it starts. But sometimes, you need a metaphorical baseball bat.

CLASSROOM CULTURE: COMPETITION

Both the complementary and symmetrical forms of schismogenesis are dependent on the function of positive feedback loops in increasing the rate and scope of change. In the case of the complementary process, the positive loops accentuate the differentiation between individuals or groups. Symmetrical schismogenesis is not so much about differentiation as it is about escalation. Two good examples of symmetrical schismogenesis are the U.S.-Soviet Cold War arms race and a baseball game. In both cases an action by one side triggers an attempt to meet or beat the action by the other side. The outcome of this process is to maintain close parity between the two sides or groups, but not necessarily by equal actions. An example of escalation of un-equals would be the civil rights movement where force was met not with force but mass; the increasing violence or resistance on one side was met by greater numbers on the other side.

In the classroom, symmetrical schismogenesis may be beneficial or detrimental depending on what is being escalated. A non-trivial example is student success or achievement. If a mediocre student, in terms of effort, is very successful on one assignment, the teacher will probably notice. If notice is all there is, and there is no feedback to the student, the student is likely to revert to pattern. However, if the teacher responds with a change in behavior, more attention, different assignments, or any other positive feedback, the student's level of effort is more likely to remain elevated, and may increase.

Part of the art of teaching is to know what kind and how much positive feedback is meaningful. If the teacher does not provide sufficient feedback, the behavior reverts. If the teacher provides too much feedback, the student may feel unable or unwilling to meet the escalation. It is as though the other team scores ten runs in the first inning.

Competition between students has a bad aroma with some teachers. And maybe it should. If not done right, it can and probably will lead to complementary schismogenesis with all the negative outcomes. However, done appropriately so that one person, group, or team does not metaphorically score ten runs in the first inning, it can generate very positive outcomes through the process of symmetrical schismogenesis.

To keep the schismogenesis symmetrical rather than complementary, the competitive situation should have the following characteristics:

- It must be limited to a specific situation, assignment, or time, and not generalized across the context. The more generalized it is, the more likely it will become complementary.
- The "rules" must be the same for all players but the outcomes may be different. In other words, you can win by running the ball or kicking the ball. If there is only one correct answer, competition tends to be complimentary and not symmetrical.
- There must be multiple, limited competitions between variable groups. Individual students competing with one another are always the same, and tend towards differentiation. Different games with different rules between different teams tend towards overall symmetry.
- The competitive situation should always be novel and unpredictable. In other words, there should be no certainty that one or another group is going to win.
- And finally, the competition must always remain a game, and be fun.

If the competition is between ephemeral groupings, and has the above characteristics, it will have much of the structure and all of the benefits of expeditionary learning. Metaphorically, competition and expeditionary learning are two sides of the same coin. Used appropriately, both not only develop the attributes of character, and increase student historicity, both increase student achievement.

CLASSROOM CULTURE: PLANNED CHANGE

Classroom culture is autopoietic, and, therefore, unique in every instance. However, the teacher is usually the single most important element in the growth, content, and function of the culture. And while the details of the culture may be unique from class to class or year to year, master teachers generally end up with cultures that "work" for them. And it is not by luck alone. Master teachers manage their classroom cultures, and change what does not work. How can the teacher carry out culture change?

Changing cultures is a complex business fraught with unintended consequences. In the classroom, the three most important sources of unintended consequences are: ignorance, or not knowing what all the involved elements are, or what their starting values are; error, not knowing all of the involved connections or interactions; and the immediate, short-term interests of the participants which may override and sabotage their long-term interests.[7]

A framework or model for managing the change process can be found in "The Concerns-Based Adoption Model" (CBAM).[8] The structure of CBAM is a series of questions about where the students are vis-à-vis the cultural change; the students' answers to these questions guide the process of change.

The first three questions are focused on what the student knows, or thinks he knows, about the change itself: What is the change? What is it supposed to do, and how does it work? What does it mean for what I do now? There is a fourth question, not listed in the literature, that must be explicitly answered: What do I lose, or what am I afraid of? These are crucial questions that, if the individual cannot answer in a way that is understood, valued, and accepted, will prevent the individual's participation or support of the change from the beginning.

Once these four questions can be answered in ways that allow change, two more questions about managing the process can be asked: Do I, the student, have the skill and knowledge to respond to this change, and make it work? After I make the change, how will I know it is working; that I am getting a benefit from the change? Again, if the answers to these questions do not give the student a high level of confidence, the innovation or change may be admired as a possibility, but never given enough support and participation to happen or succeed.

If these six questions can be answered in an acceptable manner by those participating in the change, the process of culture change is possible. It even has a good probability of success, with a lowered probability of unintended consequences because of the involvement of those experiencing the change in the guiding of the change process. In short, the process involves the many rather than the few; it precludes change by fiat. In addition, it reduces the impact of ignorance and error, and may ameliorate the impact of immediate interests.

The most immediate interests include the answers to the question of, what do I lose and what am I afraid of? The answers to this question are often the deal breakers, and can have terminal impacts on the teacher's efforts to change the class culture. It requires trust and compassion on the part of the teacher to elicit honest answers to these questions from the students. Once he has those answers, it requires competence to manage the process in such a way that twenty to thirty students are convinced they will be held harmless, or that the gain is worth a minimized pain.

CLASSROOM CULTURE: SUMMARY

We have been talking about the culture of the classroom as though it were a separate entity or subsystem within the class. However, there is no aspect or element of the class that is not modified or determined by the class culture. It is not too much of a stretch to say that the classroom culture is the class.

A teacher may be hired to teach French or Spanish, chemistry or physics, third or fourth grade. With those designations goes a certain curricular content, but it is not the content that consumes the teacher's time. The content is generally the same across the majority of schools. It has generally been taught before, many times; and if the teacher has taught it before, content may need tweaking, but rarely revamping.

It is the development and maintenance of culture that consumes the teacher's effort. In some schools, notably the military prep schools, the teacher is, officially, very constrained in the development of a unique classroom culture, and there is a striking uniformity of culture among classrooms. But even in the most uniform of schools, the details of the cultures are usually variable enough that the students, independent of the subject content, feel differently about their experience in different classes with different teachers.

A constant theme running through everything that has been written is that the goal of teaching is the increase of the student's historicity. If we artificially separate the curricular content from the culture, it is assumed that content will increase the student's technical knowledge and, thereby, his historicity. Otherwise why teach it? But this effect is dwarfed by the impact of the classroom culture. Master teachers, no matter how constrained, can shape, over time, a classroom culture that is effective, that meets the needs of the teacher and the students equally, is humane, does so without coercion, is relatively stable, does not succumb to schismogenesis, and can absorb perturbations without tearing. These are the cultures that recognize achievement and excellence in many forms, and thereby allow students to risk action to explore, change, and grow. And given a relatively safe opportunity to risk action, the students increase their self-knowledge and self-confidence. A further, but not certain, outcome of action is connection or commitment without which the student remains a squirrel. Classroom cultures enhancing the student's climb up Maslow's hierarchy assist the student in becoming fully human and fully alive.

A second theme running through much of what has been written is the idea that trust is the single most important aspect of the classroom culture. This is a trust that starts with the teacher, and is not a naïve belief that students do not lie, cheat, steal, or do any other negative action. It is a trust that the student is doing the best he knows how. It is a sorry fact in this day and age that the best he knows may include being a liar, cheater, or thief. But the teacher has the compassion and the optimism to understand that those actions are not inherent in the student. They are an overlay that can be changed; not easily and not quickly, but that's what teaching is all about. And that is what effective classroom cultures are about.

Day in day out, year in year out, master teachers have effective classroom cultures, cultures that change students. Yes, master teachers spend nights grading student work, but that is not where their hearts are. Their hearts and their brains are in the development of classroom cultures that truly grow student historicity in all its variety, complexity, and ambiguity.

NOTES

1. L. Canter, "Assertive Discipline: More than Names on the Board and Marbles in a Jar." Retrieved March 12, 2008, from http://www.humboldt .edu/~tha1/canter.html.

2. W. R. Ashby, "An Introduction to Cybernetics," 1956. Retrieved March 14, 2008, from http://www.panarchy.org/ashby/variety.1956.html.

3. R. A. Ullrich, *A Theoretical Model of Human Behavior in Organizations* (Morristown, NJ: General Learning Press, 1972).

4. G. Bateson, *Steps to an Ecology of Mind: Collected Essays in Anthropology, Psychiatry, Evolution, and Epistemology* (Chicago: University of Chicago Press, 1972).

5. P. G. Zimbardo and K. Musen, *Quiet Rage: The Stanford Prison Experiment*, motion picture (Palo Alto, CA: Stanford University, 1992). Available from http://www.prisonexp.org/.

6. "Stanford Prison Experiment." Retrieved March 14, 2008, from http://en.wikipedia.org/wiki/Stanford_Prison_Experiment.

7. R. K. Merton, "The Unanticipated Consequences of Purposive Social Action," *American Sociological Review* 1, no. 6 (1936): 894–904. Retrieved March 14, 2008, from http://www.compilerpress.atfreeweb.com/ Anno%20Merton%20Unintended.htm.

8. B. Sweeny, "The CBAM: A Model of the People Development Process," 2003. Retrieved March 14, 2008 from http://www.mentoring-association.org/membersonly/CBAM.html.

CHAPTER 5

Managing the Process

THE CLASS AS A COMPLEX ADAPTIVE SYSTEM

Teachers are, to a greater or lesser degree, free agents. They work alone. What this means in practical terms is that the master teacher must also be a master at management. I do not mean classroom management, although that is a part of it. What is meant here is the management of the organization with all it ramifications and connections to the broader environment so that it is not blindsided by what happens in or out of the class. After all, it does no good to know what you are going to teach, how you are going to teach it, and to have nurtured a classroom culture as context, and then have the whole thing be unmanaged and falling apart.

A first step toward management is to establish exactly what it is that is being managed. Simply stated, a classroom is a complex adaptive system with the following characteristics.

The first is that a class has a boundary. In order to maintain its identity, independence, and organization, it must have a boundary. The boundary may be clearly delineated, or not, but above all it must be porous because the classroom is dependent on regular inputs of material, information, and energy to survive. In addition, the boundary has to allow the export of a wide range of outputs into the classroom's environment.

Second, as a complex adaptive system, the class is made up of semi-autonomous agents including, at a minimum, the students and teacher. These agents generally act, react, and interact according to fairly simple rules, but, as a result of these actions, create an autopoietic structure with emergent properties; the sum is greater than the parts.

And the sum is often changing. Because the class contains semi-autonomous agents, it has the ability to adapt to changes in information, energy, or material flows from its environment. The response is often nonlinear and unpredictable because each agent may amplify or dampen a neighbor's response, or may respond independently of neighbors.

The history of the class is encapsulated in the rules guiding the agents' actions. This history is important because the identity of the class is found in those rules; different rules will produce a different kind of system. Therefore the rules are slow to change but precisely because they are simple, their application is ambiguous, and the agents have some autonomy. This autonomy is the source of the system's ability to adapt.

Lastly, classrooms have multiple, simultaneous functions at all times. Within the boundary, there are always at least three classes, maybe more, operating: a class for students, a class for the teacher, and a class for the community including, at least, taxpayers, parents, contractors, and, maybe, sports fans. Clearly the classes overlap, but they contain some different agents, structures, functions, and objectives; conflict is always possible.

So a class is a complex adaptive system. Okay, but what is it really? How will I know one when I see one? There are lots of possible definitions, but the easiest and most inclusive would go something like this: a class is a group of people, from at least two generations, who have come together to increase their individual and corporate historicity through a face-to-face, cooperative, adventure with no immediate pay-off. Alternatively, and less seriously, a class is a place where students learn logic, history, vocabulary, and spelling, as in the following answer to an exam question: "Abraham Lincoln became America's greatest Precedent. His mother died in infancy, and he was born in a log cabin which he built with his own hands. Abraham Lincoln freed the slaves by signing the Emasculation Proclamation."[1]

POSSIBLE MANAGEMENT METAPHORS

It is precisely the fact that classes are complex adaptive systems that gives the master teacher hope. Because they are optimists, they can, and do, work to change their class for the better.

How? The basic and most pervasive change would be to invalidate some of the common metaphors that have been applied to classrooms in order to understand and manage them. The common metaphor today is the industrial model where the class is seen as a fully automated factory, perhaps one filling cereal boxes. The students come in as flat sheets of cardboard that very early on in the process are printed and folded in a particular way to indicate the kind of box they will be and what contents they will receive as they move along a conveyor belt. Periodically, along the line there are machines that photograph and weigh the boxes. Any box that is smudged, blurry, too light, or filled with the wrong product is pushed off the belt, sometimes to be recycled, and sometimes put on a belt to the discard pile. At the end of the process, all the boxes look exactly as they should, and are filled with the expected product.

This industrial metaphor is the foundation of much that passes for education policy these days, specifically the NCLB. With this metaphor, teachers are viewed as workers on an assembly line successfully, or not, putting bits and pieces into the students as they pass through the class. Even school choice is based on the view that some schools are simply more efficient factories than others.

Is this a good metaphor? It may have some merit in its simplicity, but lacks the richness needed to absorb the variety found in any classroom. I do not think that any automated production facility is capable of absorbing the variety of inputs that classrooms do. The students arrive at the door at different developmental stages, with a variety of learning styles, with a myriad of idiosyncratic experiences and backgrounds, a wide range of familial support structures, and wildly different hopes and dreams. The belief that there is a single, best route through a class is delusional. But it is precisely this belief that produces dropout rates often, somewhere well in excess of 20 percent.

Another possible metaphor for a classroom is a circus, but that metaphor has the drawback of the spotlight shining only on the trapeze artists and the clowns. Perhaps a better metaphor for a successful classroom is a small, old-fashioned, county fair with a range of things to see and do, some nutritious, some beautiful, some fun, and some all three. At a county fair, as you go down the midway, if you turn right you may see something that changes you. If you go left, you may learn something you never even imagined. If you go straight, you may do something you know, but need to be reminded about. And what's wonderful is that your companions and informants through all this may be younger, the same age, older, or much older than you. Virtually everybody has something worth seeing, doing, or hearing. A small county fair at full tilt is a magical place on the edge of chaos, but there is an underlying order. It is not random. You can find your way; you do not have to stay lost; you can get to where you want, and see a whole lot of neat stuff on the way. County fairs are fun, exhausting, and never, ever, boring.

Not many classes live up to the metaphor of a fair. They are too sterile, too controlled. They do not contain the kinds of variety needed to be a fair, but maybe being fair-like would not be a bad target.

A BETTER METAPHOR

I have suggested two possible metaphors that might be used for describing classrooms: a factory and a county fair. They are very different in the images they conjure up. The fair is loud, dusty, odiferous, and is probably a little trashy around the edges. The factory is efficient, self-contained, and systematic. Other differences might include the following.

The factory metaphor focuses on the interior functioning of a classroom with an inherent structure largely unaffected by its environment. The structure is stable, predictable, and basically self-evident. There is a clarity and translucence that allows more confidence in a limited range of knowledge and understanding.

The fair metaphor allows elements to be fluid; the knowledge is complex, and the understanding less certain. The image of the fair is about movement and action both within the fair itself and across the boundaries. The flows of material, energy, and information from the local social fabric are crucial to the variety and richness of the fair. The image of a fair allows for change from day to day and even hour to hour. The structure is unstable, only generally predictable, and often somewhat opaque. If clarity and translucence is sought, a metaphorical Heisenberg Uncertainty Principal is revealed.

Both metaphors have their place and their fans. Much of the public and some administrators would prefer the school to be a metaphorical factory. Most students would prefer the school to be a metaphorical fair. Most master teachers would prefer a third, as yet undefined, metaphor that combines the best of both worlds. Such a metaphor would combine the stability, predictability, clarity, and translucence of the factory with the dynamism, variety, and richness of the fair.

There is a metaphor that achieves these ends. The metaphor, as developed by Stafford Beer,[2] sees any healthy organization as a viable system akin to a highly evolved vertebrate organism with the following traits:

- It will be an open, teleological, complex adaptive system able to absorb a broad range of energy, material, and informational inputs.
- To some degree, it survives internal breakdown and error or environmental change.
- It will be closely linked, competitively or cooperatively, with other systems to procure inputs and maximize outputs.
- It will coordinate and integrate a changing and changeable cast of semi-autonomous agents to maintain its identity and function far from a condition of equilibrium.
- Its viability derives from responding effectively to environmental change and surviving endogenous perturbations.
- It must be able to monitor and learn from its performance.

What is striking about this metaphor is that it is not based on any obvious similarities of content or function, as the previous two are, but rather on how information is handled by a viable classroom and an organism. Therefore, management in the broader sense I am using now is about the capture, processing, and responding to a very broad range of information from inside and outside of the classroom.

THE VIABLE TEACHER: INFORMATION SOURCES AND FLOWS

Coordination and integration in any organism is accomplished through the capture, processing, and responding to information about a difference that makes a difference.[3] In an organism, capture and response are carried out by the nerve and the endocrine systems. The two systems have similar functions, but are different; as different as a phone call and an e-mail. Both the call and the e-mail may elicit much the same response but one takes longer, lasts longer, and can carry a more complex, more nuanced message.

The messages carried by endocrine hormones are akin to the messages carried by the classroom culture. The culture shapes the class in complex ways in the same way hormones shape the body of the organism. In addition, as hormones do, the culture provides a relatively long-term, relatively stable, repertoire of responses to different sorts of information; for example, differences in student behavior and achievement, differences in teacher activities and performance, or non-threatening environmental change.

The more ephemeral flows of information are transmitted two ways: through a more formal system of short reports such as daily announcements, and calendars, akin to the autonomic nervous system, and a more informal system, including face-to-face conversations and the like, akin to the peripheral nervous system. Ephemeral does not mean forgotten. Ephemeral simply refers to the stability of the information and the length of transmission.

The autonomic portion of the system does not capture or process information; it transmits information gathered and processed by the peripheral system. It is most easily described as a "command" channel that flows from the teacher towards the students to regulate, coordinate, and moderate their actions. The autonomic system would include such things as homework assignments, grading rubrics, schedules, or the simple command to "Do this" or "Stop that."

The more informally structured, peripheral nerve system captures and responds to information from inside and outside the classroom. This is a people system. It is people who, as sensors, capture the data and decide instantly whether it might be information or not. Just as different groups of sensors will respond differently, teachers, students, and others, either as individuals or as a group, will capture different inputs.

Once the data is captured, and a decision is made that it is about a difference that makes a difference, the information travels on a ramifying network that may, or may not, include the teacher. Just as a reflex arc can operate without immediately involving the brain, a student-student capture-response network can operate absent a teacher.

All classrooms are to some extent blind because to some degree the culture defines what should be recognized as information by the sensors. For instance, gender may or may not be recognized as making a difference. There are cultures where learning differences are information, and ones where they, by themselves, are not, but the outcomes certainly are.

For the most part, these channels do not process the information they carry. With the exception of the sensor's capture decision, and the formation of the student-student reflex arc, channels are passive; they carry information but they do not assign priority, meaning, or analysis to the information. However, each type of channel—the cultural channel, the command channel, and the peripheral, capture–response channel—is uniquely capable of effectively carrying certain kinds of information, and all three are necessary to support the management functions required by a viable teacher.

THE VIABLE TEACHER: HERE-AND-NOW FUNCTION

The information that flows through the peripheral, capture-response channel is essentially an unprocessed raw material. In order to be assigned significance and meaning, it has to be processed into a context and pattern. The processing of information into a context and pattern, giving it significance and meaning, and then making a decision is what management is all about. The teacher of a viable classroom will carry out four interrelated, tightly linked, but significantly different, management functions.

The first is a here-and-now management function. This function encapsulates the common perception of what management is. This is the function that sets short-term objectives, schedules activities including field trips and assignments, assures that needed resources are available, monitors student progress, and ensures quality control. Another way of seeing this function is to say, if the class is working today, this function focuses on it working the same way tomorrow; it is about maintaining the status quo. Yet another way of describing this function is to say that it is the day-to-day classroom management familiar to all teachers.

Examples of the kinds of decisions made by this function include, but are certainly not limited to:

- What do you do when a student is sick, unable to work and absent for three days?
- What is your response to an all red, or green, eudemony meter?
- How do you deal with a shortage of textbooks?
- What do students need to know and have access to in order to do an assigned project?
- How do you handle a student who may do himself physical damage?

The last example illustrates an important point. Even though the teacher is a semi-autonomous agent in a complex adaptive system, his decisions are usually constrained by the rules or culture of a larger unit, either the school or the district. Because the rules are simple, and sometimes contravening, there is often some wiggle room but equally often there is none. If the information received by the teacher fits a particular pattern, the decision is automatic.

The information that flows to this management function is captured by the teacher either by direct observation or direct reporting by their students. These are short, high-volume channels where the variety in content is potentially huge. There must be filters that allow the teacher to focus on differences that make a difference. These filters are shaped by the rules and culture of the larger unit but they are equally idiosyncratic to the teacher.

The presence of a filter between the information source and the teacher does not mean that the teacher does not see, does not hear, or otherwise does not register the information. The filter simply classifies the information as not being about a difference important to the teacher and therefore not worth much attention. Master teachers will have filters that tend to cut volume more than variety because the variety allows the master teacher to meet the student where he is. Efforts to increase the student's historicity must be based on a high variety of information from and about the student including academic, social, and personal. Teachers focused solely on the transmission of technical knowledge will tend to have filters that cut volume and variety more or less equally; the more focused the teacher, the greater the filtration and the greater the cuts in both.

THE VIABLE TEACHER: COORDINATION

The decisions that arise from the here-and-now management function are, for the most part, about keeping the classroom on track. They are decisions about what has to be done today in response to today's situation to keep the class functioning at the highest possible level today and tomorrow; the decision horizon is rarely beyond a week and almost never more than two weeks.

There is a specialized subpart of the here-and-now function that might best be termed a coordination function involving the regulation of the students to accomplish a common objective. Coordination does not require all the students to be doing the same thing. They may or may not. Coordination is just as important in a scouting patrol through the woods as on the parade ground.

This is a management function that tracks where the students are on the road, their direction and speed, how they are doing, and the role they play in accomplishing the objective. The primary sources of information for this function are lumped together as monitoring tasks. The less formal sources of information include self-reporting by students, student comments and participation in class discussions, and, perhaps most important, student questions in and out of class.

The master teacher needs student questions the way a thirsty person needs water. If the classroom culture is such that questions are important, good questions tell the teacher where the students are, the direction they are traveling, and what they need to get there. The teacher's responses to the questions can range from restructuring class activities, through allocation of more or different resources, to simply providing a direction to move. In any case, effective responses literally link the students to the collective set of tasks the class is addressing.

The more formal sources of information include attendance sheets, homework checks, quizzes, pre- and post-tests, project progress reports, first drafts of papers, and the like. These sources, while individually informative, require record keeping in order to establish patterns that may contain far more information. We are talking grade books here.

Central to most of the patterns will be correlations, positive or negative, between the elements; say low attendance, low homework, low quiz scores; or low pretest scores, low post test scores, and high homework checks. Correlation is not causality but either of the above patterns contains more information than the simple sum of the parts and they demand improved coordination of the class activities or program.

In larger organizations, the here-and-now and the coordination functions are often undertaken by different individuals; the product manager versus the shop foreman; the head of school versus the registrar. In the classroom, the teacher does both. The point to be made here is that the coordination function feeds the here-and-now function information as the basis for decisions made to be carried out by the coordination function. In most hierarchies, coordination is a staff function whereas the here-and-now is a command function. The coordination function is very important but has no independent decision-making ability outside of the parameters set by the here-and-now. Independence would mean the administrative assistant was running the company.

THE VIABLE TEACHER: EXTERNAL-AND-FUTURE FUNCTION

If the teacher is a master at the here-and-now management function, and if there is nobody better at coordination, the class will be an island of stability and effectiveness in an environment on the edge of chaos; but not for long. It is precisely because the environment is constantly changing in unpredictable ways that the teacher has to manage the external-and-future.

This is a research-and-development function that instead of asking, are we meeting our objectives, asks are we meeting the needs of a student; are these the best objectives? And if they are the best, are we meeting them in the best possible way? This is a Janus-faced function. It faces outwards constantly scanning the environment for nascent trends that will make a difference. It faces inwards constantly questioning the operations within the class. In short, this function is about change.

Much of the information supporting this function comes to teachers the same way it comes to everybody else; via journals,

newspapers, books, conversations with the neighbors, and just being aware of what's happening in and around the neighborhood.
The more specialized information about possible changes in education in general, and their school in particular, comes to them
through professional development, union meetings, faculty meetings, hallway conversations with their principals, and the give and
take of the teachers' lounge. This may be the only thing that guar-
antees teachers talking to each other.

The actual information tends to be fragmented, incomplete, contradictory, and buried in a high volume of meaningless noise. There
is a great deal of sifting that has to be done to place the information
into patterns that make sense. This sifting and patterning has to happen outside of the class. It cannot be done in front of twenty-plus
students. It might need an evening in front of the fire, or a weekend.
As will the second step, reflecting on the operations and objectives
of the classroom in light of the patterns and their implications.

In larger organizations, where the here-and-now and the external-
and-future management functions are separate entities, the external-
and-future function is limited to asking questions, developing possible answers and making suggestions to the here-and-now function.
This is not a command function; it cannot demand change. It has to
persuade and negotiate to bring about the organizational change it
wants.

For teachers, who do it all in one brain, all the negotiations are in
the form of an internal dialogue between alter egos; the adventurer
on one shoulder shouting, "change," and the stay-at-home on the
other saying, "steady." Master teachers tend to listen to the stay-at-
home while hearing the adventurer. The trick is not to exceed the
limited capacity of the class to absorb change. Every organization,
classrooms included, needs a recovery period, called relaxation time,
after every change. The greater the change the longer the relaxation
time until the classroom stabilizes into a new pattern. If changes are
attempted at too rapid a pace, the new patterns are never found and
the class slides towards instability and chaos.

There is one area in which the external-and-future management function should reign supreme: the creation and re-creation of the filters that winnow the information flows to the here-and-now function. Again, the filters cannot change too often or too much too fast, but they have to change as frequently as the inherent rate of change in the classroom. If they do not, the disparities between what actually happens in class and what gets through the filter will steadily increase. The management function must have a level of variety equal to the system managed. The external-and-future management function is about engineering sufficient variety so the here-and-now remains effective.

THE VIABLE TEACHER: THE IDENTITY FUNCTION

There is often a tension between the here-and-now and the external-and-future management functions. Sometimes what one function thinks is a really good idea, the other function feels will not work for equally good reasons. This kind of impasse cannot be resolved by the two functions. They are both doing the best they know how, and they are both convinced of the correctness of their positions. What is required is an arbiter who is neither of the functions; an arbiter who is larger than either, and subsumes both.

The arbiter in this case is an identity function that answers, for the teacher, the questions of who I am, what do I know and believe, and what do I value? In short, this function is an expression of the teacher's historicity. The identity function is by far the most complex of the four management functions. Every statement made earlier about the student's historicity is equally true of the teacher's historicity.

For beginning teachers, *qua* teacher, their historicity is largely a function of what was learned or inherited from the master teachers they experienced. As such it is largely unexamined; these questions of who and what do not have explicit, generalized answers. The answers that do exist are developed in response to specific issues and challenges as they arise. Over time, with experience and reflection, the answers tend to coalesce into a pattern. This pattern represents the individual's attributes of character or persona, *qua* teacher, both inside the class and in the broader context.

For the more experienced teacher, the primary source of information for this identity function is an intellectual construct or vision of what teaching should be and a road map to how he can approach this vision. The information that supports the construction of this vision comes from both the here-and-now and the external-and-future management functions. In the early and, perhaps, middle part of a career, the vision is fluid and can change, but as history accrues, the vision becomes more fully developed, and more resistant to change.

Difficult to change or not, most visions are not explicit. A characteristic of master teachers is that they have explicit visions. In most cases they have written, rewritten, and then written out their visions again until they say exactly what they mean. Often, a part of the hiring process in independent schools is the requirement that the candidate present a philosophy of education. Most candidates hope that their schooling, experience, and recommendations will get them the job. And they may. But all of that is ephemeral, and becomes less and less important with every passing day.

What remains with the teacher, even as it changes, is the statement of vision or philosophy that provides the pole star to their career and allows them to make all the difficult, ambiguous choices between change and no change. And in the melee of teaching, it constantly calls for them to move personally and professionally in a given direction.

THE VIABLE TEACHER: FUNCTIONAL BALANCE

Four management functions, each important, each requiring a slightly different perspective, all being done by a single person; sometimes it does get complicated. But what saves all teachers from serious trouble is that one function, the here-and-now including co-ordination, takes up, perhaps as an estimate, 90 percent of their time, effort, and thought. The second function, the external-and-future, takes up, perhaps, seven or eight percent of their management effort with the remaining two or three percent going to the identity function. The functions are all equally important but they are not equally consuming of that rarest commodity, time.

Nor do all four functions have to be done at the same exact moment. No teachers develop a vision of education or teaching while standing in front of a class of thirty expectant students. Nor do they do much of their research and development at that moment. Both of these management functions are mostly done when the class is not in session; both functions are done during the evenings, weekends, vacations and the summer because both require a commitment of time to study, formally or informally, and to reflect on experience.

The teachers who achieve an appropriate balance between the four functions and manage to do them all are easily recognized; they are the master teachers.

They have robust classes capable of absorbing the slings and arrows of outrageous fortune; the class has a stability that the students know and appreciate. Students may, or may not, like the class but they are comfortable with the way the class is run; to them, the class itself is transparent. Students feel they understand how the class works and what the expectations are. In short, they see the teacher as competent.

More important, the students have the feeling that the teacher knows who they are. The teacher sees them, hears them, and understands them. They are free to talk to the teacher about what they do, how they do it, and what they need to get it done. And the teacher responds to them as individuals by being open to change and moving the system to meet their needs. In short, the students see the teacher as compassionate.

The students of these teachers never wonder why they are doing the things they are doing. There is always a connection between the class and the world. The connection is never, you need this to get into college, and rarely, you need this to get a job. The connection is always, you need this if you are going to intervene in, and take control of your own life. In short, the students see the teacher as having relevant life experience.

These are the teachers who get up almost every morning ready to teach. They are confident in what they are doing and where they are going. To use a cliché, these are the teachers who, when waist deep in crocodiles, clearly remember that they came in to drain the swamp. Confidence is not arrogance. They recognize that on any given day, in any given place, another teacher might be doing a better job; there is always something to learn and somebody to teach them. They have a personal security, *qua* teacher, that allows them to take the best from others and use it to grow as a teacher without losing their own persona.

These are the teachers with the technical knowledge, the social and fiscal capital, and the worldview to intervene in their own classrooms to move toward their vision of teaching. These are the teachers that other teachers tend to admire, students tend to respect and trust, parents tend to appreciate, and administrators will kill for.

THE NONVIABLE TEACHER

But what happens if an appropriate balance is not maintained? The short answer is that it gets ugly. If one of the management functions is short-changed, both the teacher, *qua* teacher, and the class lose their viability.

If the management of the here-and-now is insufficient the class does not flow; it moves in a herky-jerky fashion with periods of inactivity followed by periods of frenetic activity. Coordination of activities will be a sometimes thing, and the actions and achievements of the students will be unmonitored and largely unknown.

If, on the other hand, the here-and-now is all there is, the teacher will use, over and over again, unexamined, yellowed lecture notes from years ago. He can do the whole segment from memory. He has the here-and-now down pat; he knows how long it takes, what he is going to say, and what he expects to happen. He does not need to prepare; he can just wing it. There is little or nothing that is new, vibrant, exciting, or, perhaps, relevant to today. Both he and the students are bored, and just grinding through the material.

A failure to effectively manage the external-and-future can wreak havoc on the filters available to the teacher. Unexamined and unrefreshed filters will, over time, degrade, and allow less and less variety through. The insufficient, almost monochromatic filter can diminish and compress the class into a dry husk of a thing with little or no communication and even less trust. Without a proper external-and-future function, the class will become increasingly focused on the internal logic of what is studied, without paying attention to how the knowledge gained will be useful to the students' future lives. It is the external function that answers questions of the utility of what is learned; without it, material is learned just because it is there.

Too great a focus on the external-and-future function degrades the students' trust in the class in two ways. First, students become uncertain and insecure because the rate of change exceeds their recovery rate, and they do not know how the class works, what is important, or what is expected. Much of what they do will appear arbitrary and disconnected. Second, if the teacher is viewed as seeking external validation, the students will question if they are evaluated on their performance in class, or on some aspect of their life outside of class.

One of the fundamental rules of cybernetics is that unused information quickly becomes unusable; it becomes unstable, degraded, and inapplicable. If the identity function is not upgraded, refreshed, and referred to on a regular basis, it cannot function as a lode star. A teacher with a degraded identity function is a teacher going through the motions and not doing much else. It's tough to get up in the morning, and there is little or no joy brought to the class when he arrives. The loss of a vision means the loss of any reason for working hard to be an effective, much less a master, teacher. What is left can range from numbness to a biting cynicism.

The common term for this situation is "burnout" often characterized by:

> (1) some degree of physical and emotional exhaustion; (2) socially dysfunctional behavior, particularly a distancing and insulation from individuals with whom one is working; (3) psychological impairment—especially strong, negative feelings toward the self; and (4) organizational inefficiency through decreased output and poor morale.[4]

In the worst cases, the teacher may not be breaking any rules, but he is killing curiosity, crushing enthusiasm, poisoning excitement, and eviscerating morale. This is a teacher who has moved past being nonviable, and is a member of the living dead, a zombie.

TEACHER BURNOUT

Burnout is one of the open secrets of teaching. It's a little like the flu. Everybody gets it from time to time, especially in February, and I doubt that there are very many teachers who are not burned out in June. And like the flu, it seems highly contagious, but it's more a bother than a threat to most. Unfortunately, for some, especially the youngest, least experienced, most idealist, and the oldest, closest to retirement teachers, burnout can be fatal to a career.

Burnout is strongly associated with long-term stress. Teaching is structurally a stressful job. Teachers must be constantly "up," responsive to, and prepared for whatever the students present them with. They need to be constantly aware, and have eyes in the back of their heads. The ambiguity of expectations and priorities, the frequent lack of administrative support when push comes to shove, the out-of-class demands with the responsibilities that often are neither paid for nor appreciated, the isolation from others, and the feeling that problems and solutions suggested are problems and solutions ignored, can all raise the levels of stress for teachers. In addition, teachers, like students, are at the beck and call of bells and whistles that are often arbitrary and unconnected to what's happening at the moment.

On a more personal level, you pour your heart and soul into a lesson, put yourself out in front of a very tough audience, and after everything is said and done, you have no good idea whether you made any real difference. Sure, the multiple-guess tests may show that you filled the cereal boxes, but is that the only thing that counts? Or you crawl out on a limb to rescue a student, and he turns to spit in your eye. Or, you set up a creative exercise involving student teams, and your principal gets an earful from parents who do not like what you are doing; how will their students get full credit for their own work? On the cosmic scale of things, these issues do not loom large. But neither do the individual grains on a piece of sandpaper; it's just that there are so doggone many of them.

The broader, social sources of burnout are the frustrations inherent in teaching. Every teacher out there started out thinking something was important; the students, the subject, the job, or all three. But as they taught, they discovered that, apparently, others did not agree with them. Look at school facilities: older schools look like derelict factories, and many of the newer ones are hard to distinguish from low-security prisons. How many other equally important social functions are dependent on bake sales or the generosity of the workers to make ends meet? What other social service organizations are so often directed by politically motivated boards, many with agendas having nothing to do with children? Does any other profession, except possibly lawyers, get cast as scapegoats as often as teachers? But then, most lawyers earn more money than teachers, and that sends a very different message.

Earning a living is likely to be a tough business. Teaching is a tough business. Over 50 percent, sometimes up to 95 percent, of new teachers quit in less than five years; the average teaching career lasts only eleven years for the 58 percent of newly certified teachers with the courage to take the first job. Burnout and stress cost society, teachers, and students unconscionable amounts of time, money, effort, efficacy, and pain.[5]

EARLY STAGE BURNOUT

The symptoms of the early stages of burnout are all about "lacks," and might include a lack of energy, joy, enthusiasm, satisfaction, motivation, interest, zest, dreams for life, ideas, concentration, permission to play, self-confidence, and humor. Full-blown burnout can have serious medical implications and symptoms ranging from persistent anxiety to thoughts of possible suicide.[6]

Early stage, mild bouts of burnout are a recurring theme in teachers' professional lives. February is a month when burnout seems endemic; the year stretches out in front of you, the skies are cold and gray, and the old cliché of "when you are waist deep in alligators, it is hard to remember that you are trying to drain the swamp" fits perfectly. A cure for this stage of burnout might include the following:

Get real. Yes, you are a teacher but that is not all you are. At best, the school only pays enough to buy about a third of your life. Do not tie your identity to the classroom and teaching. Get a hobby. Get a balance between all your parts. Talk to people who are not teachers. Remember that the world is bigger and better than your classroom, and you are but a part of that world.

Relax. If you have done your best, you do not owe anybody an apology. You cannot be expected to single-handedly change, protect, or mend a student, the school, or the world. You can make a difference, and you can and should rejoice in that fact without becoming delusional about your abilities to be perfect, omniscient, or omnipotent.

Rest. Burnout is about psychological and physical exhaustion. I do not necessarily mean go to bed, although that might be a good idea. I mean give it a rest. Do not take stuff home; leave it at school. It'll be there when you return. When you are away from school, leave it alone, and stop thinking about it. Instead read a romance or a western. But whatever you do, do it at your own rhythm. You've got too many bells at school. Do not tolerate too many at home.

Plan. The urgent always drives out the important. Urgency comes from deadlines. Some deadlines are real, but many are just convenient. If you can only get two things done today, make sure at least one is important to you away from school. When you plan, prioritize. Try to get to the first priorities; think about the second priorities; and forget the thirds. If they have merit, they will return to your desk later, and you can deal with them then.

Change. The kiss of death is to do today what you did yesterday just because that's what you did before. Look around; there are a hundred different, exciting ways of doing what you do. Examples are all around you. Try one of them; see how it works. Maybe it's better; maybe it's not, but in any case, you have broken a deadening routine and learned something new. The change may be large or small, a change of school, grade, subject, or wardrobe. But what that change cannot do is add to your load. If you are going to add, then you must drop.

Laugh. You have to laugh, I mean a really healthy laugh, at least once every day. It may not happen at school. It would be nice if it did, but it has to happen somewhere. And it would be better if it were shared with someone.

When you get real, relax, rest, plan, change, and laugh, you are on your way back; burnout is not likely to continue or progress any farther.

LATE STAGE BURNOUT

Sometimes, in spite of every effort, early, mild burnout progresses to late, end stage, full-blown burnout. If this happens, radical change is called for. The chances that the teacher can fully recover, while teaching, seem to be very slim. Radical change is tough. Let's assume for the moment that the burned-out teacher has decided that the kind of vision he started with is gone and he needs to do something else. Often, experienced teachers, ones with a decade or more in the classroom, are afraid that they are not really qualified to do anything but teach.

Hello?! Has anyone been paying attention for the last seventy pages or so? Teaching is an incredibly complex business requiring a broad range of talents to do well. Anyone who has ever approached excellence or effectiveness as a teacher has a fair amount of historicity. After all, independent of what year or subject they teach, teachers have a great deal of technical information including a repertoire of practical, applied skills across the fields of recruitment, leadership, management, training, and motivation. In addition, they have at least some social and fiscal capital to underwrite a new intervention. The only element they lack is the worldview that gives meaning to what they are doing now, teaching.

They need to develop a new vision, to discover a new meaning supported by the technical knowledge and skills that they may, or may not, realize they have. There are whole bookshelves of books telling you how to change careers. Many of them have interesting things to say and it is worth exploring them. In addition, a search of the Web will call up sites from universities, colleges, and others with information about alternative careers for teachers.

There is one book, *Don't Retire, Rewire*,[7] that, even though the authors never use the term, is a practical handbook on exploring one's historicity, developing a new vision, and identifying the skills that the individual has to support that vision. The book talks about creating a new career after retirement, but the techniques are equally valid for anyone with a decade or so of teaching. However, the book is written for, and focuses on, individuals who are in the process of really significant change from one type of career to an entirely different type of career. That may not be the only option for the burned-out teacher.

It may be that a burned-out teacher can develop a new vision simply by changing contexts. There are lots of opportunities for teachers who do not fit the traditional context of the mainstream, main-line, American classroom. The range of jobs involving teaching out-side of the standard classroom is huge. Every age group, every sub-ject, every type of audience, and every sort of approach is found. The very act of exploring the wide range of options, opportunities, and possibilities is good for morale. The trapped feeling disappears.

Many of the jobs will not pay as well as teaching in the usual classroom setting; some pay significantly more, especially in some of the overseas jobs off the beaten track.

Be that as it may, there is no reason that a seriously burned-out teacher has to struggle to continue being a regular teacher in a regu-lar classroom in a regular school. The quality of life is inherently higher when the three elements of historicity are mutually support-ive. When the knowledge and skills available, the social and fiscal capital are sufficient, and the worldview and vision give meaning, life is good. When one or more of the elements are out of step, life is less wonderful and far more stressful.

SAUCE FOR THE GOOSE, SAUCE FOR THE GANDER

Burnout is an inherent problem whenever one or more of the fol-lowing are present: a surfeit in the number and complexity of social interactions, ambiguity of expectations, an inability to control what happens, a perceived shortfall of resources, a dull, repetitive pattern, and a desire to do well.

Burnout is inherent in teaching. It is a real problem and a whole lot of effort has been made to understand the etiology, progression, and amelioration of the "teachers' disease." But like the flu, burnout can strike anybody in the classroom. Any teacher who uses the term "burnout" has to be willing to apply it not only to them-selves and other teachers but equally to their students; even their kindergarteners.[8]

Students are subject to many, if not all, the stressors that teachers are subject to but do not have the experience or the skills to handle them. Therefore, they may suffer burnout more quickly than adults believe possible. The symptoms of student burnout may depend on the age of the student.

For younger students, the symptom of choice is anger. This may be expressed in the youngest by a tantrum. Slightly older students may just say, "It's not fair!" They are angry about everything and nothing is fair.

After students have made an initial effort, withdrawal may be a symptom of burnout. "I cannot get it done, so I will not try." "I'm too dumb to do this." "Nobody likes me; everybody hates me." If these are attitudes and not just statements made in a moment of frustration, the student has been overwhelmed and short-circuited by the situation.

The symptoms of burnout in high school students are similar to the adult symptoms except that they develop more quickly as burnout may progress more quickly. Sometimes burned-out students are diagnosed as depressed and, indeed, they may be depressed. Some writers, in fact, call burnout "job depression."[9] But if the students have not been depressed in the past and they suddenly are, they may be exhibiting burnout. Many of the symptoms may be the same; the source and the cure may not be necessarily the same.

The cure for burned-out high school students is very much the same as it is for teachers, with one huge difference. Because of their inexperience and their position in the school, teenagers need permission and support from adults, including their teachers, to address their burnout; they do not have the power to make the needed decisions.

In cases of early, mild burnout, the teacher is an appropriate source of assistance by giving the student permission and options to get real, relax, rest, plan, change, exercise, and laugh. In more severe cases, the appropriate response comes primarily from parents with the assistance of the teacher. In the worst-case scenarios, neither parents nor teachers are competent to handle the situation. Serious professional counseling is called for; virulent burnout is dangerous to the student's health. It may lead to extreme risk-taking, drug abuse, and possible suicide.

Teacher burnout is recognized as a pervasive issue in the K–12 classroom. K–12 student burnout may be, probably is, just as big and, may be, bigger. The tragedy is nobody seems to know.

NOTES

1. The British Council, "Funny Exam Answers" (Number 23). Retrieved March 14, 2008, from http://www.britishcouncil.org/learnenglish-central-stories-exams.htm.

2. This discussion of management is very loosely based on the Viable Systems Model developed by Stafford Beer in *The Brain of the Firm 2nd ed.* (1994) and *The Heart of Enterprise* (1994) both available as a special print from John Wiley & Sons.

3. G. Bateson, *Mind and Nature: A Necessary Unity* (Toronto: Bantam Books, 1988), 105.

4. A. Cedoline, excerpt from "Job Burnout in Public Education: Symptoms, Causes, and Survival Skills," 1982. Retrieved March 14, 2008, from http://smhp.psych.ucla.edu/qf/burnout_qt/what_is_burnout.pdf.

5. M. Haberman, "Teacher Burnout in Black and White," 2004. Retrieved March 14, 2008 from http://www.ednews.org/articles/584/1/Teacher-Burnout-in-Black-and-White/Page1.html.

6. "Three Stages of Burnout." Retrieved March 14, 2008, from http://smhp.psych.ucla.edu/qf/burnout_qt/3stages.pdf.

7. J. Sedlar and R. Miners, *Don't Retire, Rewire!* (Indianapolis: Alpha Books, 2003). Also available from http://dontretirerewire.com/.

8. K. Herrera, "Teachers Dismiss Long Day Proposal," 2006. Retrieved March 14, 2008, from http://www.smdp.com/article/articles/1066/1/Teachers-dismiss-long-day-proposal/print/1066.

9. B. Potter, "Job Burnout; What It Is & What You Can Do About It," 2005. Retrieved March 14, 2008, from http://www.docpotter.com/art_bo-summary.html.

CHAPTER 6

Beyond the Classroom

TEACHER AND PARENTS

As a group, teachers and parents have an approach-avoidance reaction to each other. There is no question that supportive parents are the greatest boon that a teacher can have. And I think that the approbation of parents is more meaningful to teachers than almost any other reward the teacher can receive.

However, the parent and teacher are sometimes working at cross-purposes. If the goal of teaching is to increase the student's historicity, then the teaching is about increasing the student's technical knowledge and skills base, increasing his social capital, and developing his worldview. Virtually all parents in the world would support increasing their students' historicity. That's precisely what they want, but not at the expense of goring the parent's sacred cows.

In my experience, parents want their children to be just like them, only more so. They want them to be as successful, only more so. They want them to be as good citizens, only more so. They want them to understand the world as they do, only more so. If parents feel that the teacher is ineffective and not doing enough for their student to be "more so," they will complain and fight. These fights are not emotional battles. They are disagreements about degrees of difference and can be settled relatively easily by negotiation, compromise, and time.

But parents are very uncomfortable with a redefinition of success, citizenship, or understanding. Of these, parents are most sensitive to changes in the understanding of the world because that is based on a worldview. The individual's worldview is just about a definition of who the individual is. To have one's child taught in a manner that calls into question one's worldview is a serious threat to almost all parents.

If parents feel their worldview is undercut or abrogated by the teacher, there are two common responses: retreat to guerrilla warfare or full frontal assault. Of the two, the more common seems to be a guerrilla warfare defined as complaints to the school administration about secondary issues that implicitly challenge the parent's worldview. A full frontal assault is complaints to the board or legal actions. In both cases, there is a major emotional component to the argument; a threatened parent is an emotional parent.

The fact that the teacher is essentially a free agent complicates the relationship because the parents generally are getting their information through the lens of the student, a lens that may be distorted by inexperience or by self-interest. But let it be said, if the student lens distorts what is happening in class, that fact, in and of itself, may be indicative of ineffective teaching. The teacher has not made clear the why, what, or how he is doing in a way that makes sense to the student.

Because teaching is about increasing the student's historicity, there will always be the potential for conflict precisely because the teacher's actions move the locus of control away from the parent towards the student. To the extent that there is a difference in worldviews, the potential for conflict increases because the differences will lead to different expressions of the attributes of character and different ways of being, or becoming, fully human and fully alive. Even though students will often take proactive actions to protect their teacher, parent-teacher conflict is inherent in effective teaching. Conflict may be ameliorated by effective teaching, but there is nothing placid about being a master teacher.

TEACHER AND HOME VISITS

Since parent-teacher conflict is inherent in effective teaching, what prevents the onset of symmetrical schismogenesis? How can the teacher prevent a minor disagreement from escalating to a full-blown confrontation? As is often the case, the answer is a cliché, but the answer is to create a partnership between the teacher and the parent by establishing a dialogue between the two.

Perhaps the most effective communication between a teacher and a parent is a student going home feeling excited, successful, and confident about what happened in class that day. If this is the only link, there is the danger of a lack of memory. What if the student goes home bored, unsuccessful, and lacking confidence? The message of the moment tends to be extrapolated into the past and the future.

The cure for this kind of volatility is redundancy, having multiple communication channels independent of the student. The richest, most redundant, channels of communication are face-to-face meetings between the parent and teacher. This sort of communication happens formally on conference days, back-to-school nights, or the like, and informally at athletic events, on the sidewalks after school, and the like. Such meetings are limited by time but if they happen often enough, they can be very valuable. However, their value is limited by the fact that these are comfortable venues for the teacher and uncomfortable venues for the parents. The teacher is at home, and the parent is not.

For teachers, the scariest, most uncomfortable, and potentially most valuable meeting with parents will take place during a home visit. Home visits are a required part of Head Start programs, more common in elementary schools, and rare but growing in high schools. Certainly home visits are less scary if they are part of a school-wide program and the teachers have received some training for them. But even if the school has not instituted such a program, teachers can initiate the visits on their own, if only on a limited scale.

A teacher contemplating a home visit should keep the following points in mind.

- Overwhelmingly, parents appreciate the visit and have a positive response to the teacher.

- Teachers can visit as pairs, but that increases the possibility of overwhelming the parents.
- Some just ring the door bell; usually a poor idea. Send a letter in advance with a light tone about getting acquainted and not judging or evaluating. No preparation is required. Our homes need to be vacuumed and we are on diets![1]
- If home is not an option, find a neutral ground where you can share a cup of coffee, on you.
- Be prepared but not committed to an agenda. The best conversations are autopoietic and take time to develop.
- A visit towards the start of the year is about goals and potentials and not about problems.
- A visit is never about problems, it is always about increasing achievement with solutions developed with and by the parents. The first question should be a variant of how can I help?
- Don't sit there taking voluminous notes, but if there is follow-up, then follow up.
- Do not be in a hurry, but do not overstay your welcome.

Home visits are a powerful and unique tool for teachers. They are powerful simply because of the volume of information that is exchanged and they are unique in that the volume is heaviest from parent to teacher rather than from teacher to parent. Home visits have the potential to change the teacher, the student, and the parents.

TEACHER AND PARENTAL COMMUNICATION

A second short circuit of conflict between parents and teachers is the realization on the part of teachers that if parents will not fight for their kids, who will? The trick is to give parents the information they need to fight effectively, and not waste time tearing down straw men of their own or others' making.

If it is available, and often it is not, technology gives the teacher a powerful way of communicating with parents. The easiest, simplest way of using technology is to e-mail parents. I have seen several teachers beset with parental woes defuse the situation simply by producing a weekly Friday newsletter for all parents about what happened in the previous week and what is coming up in the next week. The teachers took the opportunity to discuss, without identifying individual students, what had been successful and what needed a little more work. In every case, the parents stopped complaining and became more involved in the classes. All the parents wanted to know was where the class was going and how the teacher thought it would get there. They were very appreciative of the fact that the teacher could and would change the program when students were having difficulties.

Obviously, if a student is struggling in the class, a weekly bulletin to the parents will prevent surprises at the end of the grading period and provides an opportunity for taking collective remedial actions to support the student.

E-mails are efficient but require extra steps to keep track of. An easier way of doing things is to establish a classroom blog. A blog, or more formally a Web log, is an online journal available to anybody with an Internet connection or limited to only select readers. Most blogs written by teachers are about teaching in general and their experience in particular but there are class-specific blogs out there. The glory of blogs is that they are very flexible; a teacher can post as often and as long as he likes. The blog can be a forum with an open conversation between parents and teacher, or it can limit the comments entirely and have parents directly contact the teacher through e-mail.

Blogs started as the dynamic elements in the more static Web page format. Designing a Web page is more complex a task than starting a blog, but it has the advantage of relative permanence. It is a good place for long-term policies and announcements. Producing a frequently updated blog within a stable Web page combines the best of all possible worlds; both fundamental policies and day-to-day operations are readily available to the parents.

The Web page–blog setup is very effective but "Moodle"[2] may be making this approach increasingly obsolete. Moodle is an open source program that allows students and parents to get the class assignments, class activities, and to some extent class discussions online. In addition it can be set up so the students can see their grades as they are posted. The potential for making the class transparent seems huge, but I have to say that my present position on Moodle is analogous to a new car buyer. I've taken it for a short test ride and understand some of the features, but have not yet really put it through its paces for any real length of time. People I respect say that it is the wave of the future; I am hopeful it will reduce conflict, but when does more become less? When does clarity increase conflict rather than reduce it?

TEACHER AND PARENT HISTORICITY

If parents will not fight for their kids, who will? Sometimes the parent-teacher conflict arises because it is the teacher who stands up for the student. Most experienced teachers can tell stories of parents who have robbed a child of the opportunity to explore, learn, and construct a self during childhood. We all know stories about the Little League Father or the Stage Mother, parents who dominate and drive their children to achieve the parent's dreams. Less well known are the Academic Achievers who believe that what one does in kindergarten determines one's life. I had a parent of a senior tell me that if his son did not get into Princeton, his son would not, could not, get a good job, and would be doomed to mediocrity for the rest of his life. This was an honestly held opinion before the event, not a pity party in the face of failure. But this idea did not come close to rationality. Imagine how potentially harmful it was to the student involved.

Equally damaging is the Comparison Shopper who constantly compares one sibling with another. The older child excels in math and science; why does the second child waste so much time with the arts? If he is going to be successful like his sister, he must take a second year of calculus. If he does not, he is going to be less than her.

What unifies the Little League Father, Stage Mother, Academic Achiever, and Comparison Shopper is that they all want too much control of the student's historicity. Since teaching is about increasing the student's historicity, the teacher has to attempt neutralizing their impact. I say attempt because the teacher cannot just say, "That's the dumbest thing I have ever heard." If he does that, he becomes a second or third parent, and a part-time one at that, competing for control of the student's historicity. The student is placed in the position of choosing the teacher over the parents. Most of the time he will choose the parents, and nothing much will change.

Often the issue arises because of the inherent conservatism of parents regarding their child. The parents are basing their perceptions on their own history and what they know. In this case, the teacher has to broaden the parents' horizons; to point out that Bill Gates, G. W. Bush, and lots of other successful people did not go to Princeton. But this is a rational argument and rationality does not always work in the face of fear. A more successful approach would be to use a modified CBAM approach with a focus on addressing what the parents fear. It will take time to piece together the answer because one cannot just walk up to parents and ask the question outright. Once having the answer, the teacher may be able to help parents, not to make decisions and judgments about what the student is doing, but rather to ask questions including, but not limited to:

What are your dreams and goals or who do you want to be?
Do you have a plan?
Do you have a plan B?
What are the benefits of your plans?
What are the social, fiscal, and lost opportunity costs of your plan?

It is unlikely that most students can start by effectively answering these questions to anyone's satisfaction. But now both the teacher and the parents, working together, have a target to aim for; helping the student develop his own, albeit tentative, answers and taking more control of his own historicity.

TEACHING AND NATIONAL POLITICS

Since the overarching goal of teaching is to increase the student's historicity, his ability to effectively intervene in his own life and, perhaps, in the lives of others, then teaching is a political act, and the teacher, perforce, must take political stands.

I do not mean that teachers must participate in partisan political activity or be a Republican or Democrat. I do mean that teachers must exert expert leadership to society in issues of education, nationally and locally.

Nationally, teachers will be able to provide leadership only if they band together. Some will say they already have done so in their unions such as the NEA. But unions are not the answer. Unions are focused on teachers and not education. Unions have served a useful purpose in getting better salaries and improving working conditions. Often they make the claim that what they do benefits students, but that is a side effect. The focus is on the benefit for the teacher. Too often a union protects a teacher who really should not be teaching, and the unions have lost credibility with parents, the community, and opinion-shapers whenever they actually might speak for education.

There are lots of specialized, teacher associations for every content area found in the school. If you read their mission statements, the focus of these groups tends to be very narrow and does not encompass all of K–12 education. In times of shortages, they may compete for resources.

The only national association with the interests of students at heart is the PTA. But the PTA is primarily the parents' perspective on the local school. This is valuable, but is not a way for teachers to be heard. Teachers must cede the dominant voice in the PTA because they are employed by the school system. Further, teachers and parents often have conflicting goals and ideas about what education can and should be.

Teachers should learn from doctors. The first hundred or so years of the AMA were pretty much focused on raising the standards and definitions of both doctors and medical treatment. In 1847, doctors were not professionals; just about anybody could claim to be a doctor and just about any quackery could be called medicine. In a relatively short time, the AMA turned doctors from quacks into folk heroes in white coats.

Teachers need the same kind of make over. They need to wrest control of their professional definition away from those who know virtually nothing about what it means to teach. Teachers, not parents, politicians, or corporations, should define what it means to be a teacher, in terms of qualifications, actions, and outcomes. Now before everybody gets excited, I need to make two points and ask two questions. The first point is that teachers do not need what the AMA has become in the last fifty years, basically a powerful lobbyist group focused on the well-being of doctors. The second point is that the broader society can, and should, always set the heuristic goals of their educational systems. To do otherwise is to grant inappropriate power to teachers.

Finally, there are two questions to be asked. The first question is, if we gave any one of the high stakes tests such as the SAT, ACT, or NCLB mandated state tests to a thousand congressmen, CEO's, artists, or military officers, would a significant portion be embarrassed by their performance? Which raises the second question, what does a successful person need to know, and how and where can each person learn it?

The answers to these last questions should drive a national organization of teachers. Forget the rest of it. If we can get this in front of the nation, everything else will come.

TEACHING AND LOCAL POLITICS

Not every teacher wants to, or should, or can provide educational leadership to the local community. To lead the community in a thoughtful conversation about education, teachers need to have the following characteristics:

They must

- have a clear vision of what teaching and education might be;
- take pride and joy in being a teacher;
- understand and respect, even admire, most of the surrounding society and culture;
- have expertise, compassion, and life experience;
- not be defensive, and they cannot have an arrogant bone in their body.

In short they have to be master teachers or be on their way to becoming one. But not every master teacher can provide local leadership. Doing so requires a significant commitment of thought, time, and interest, on top of the daily teaching load.

In more cases than not, it is through conversation that leadership happens. Almost 70 percent of Americans have access to the Internet.[3] That number is rapidly increasing, although not uniformly across the board, and by using the Internet, teachers can easily have a two-way, multipart conversation with the surrounding community. The vehicle for this conversation is the teacher's professional blog.

A teacher's blog may be a hugely sophisticated enterprise or it can be the soul of simplicity. There are thousands of models to look at already on the Web. For a start, search with the string, "education blog listing." Most of the listed blogs are either very personal journals or reports of the happenings and activities of a single classroom. Fewer blogs aspire to a national audience and have thousands of hits every day. There are many regional blogs but there seem to be few or no education blogs targeting a more limited geographic area; be it a district, town, or city. The regional education blog is an unexplored niche that could have a huge impact, all out of proportion to the time and effort expended.

Once a teacher has decided to create a blog, setting up an effective blog should take him less than ten minutes; the technical aspects are not onerous.[4] Once it is up and running, talk it up, announce it, and spread the word amongst present and past parents.

It's not the technology that is difficult, it is the follow-through. First, blogs thrive on a pattern. You do not have to post every day but you have to post regularly; every Friday, or whatever. You can take announced breaks but you cannot randomize the pattern. Your post is not a magnum opus; we're talking one, two, three paragraphs or a short introduction and link to another's blog or newspaper article. This is, after all, a conversation; not a lecture. You want your post to generate comments and responses that you, and others, can respond to.

The writing does not have to be formal; again it's a conversation, but please read and reread and read again what you post. Spelling and grammar, if not correct from a teacher, is disconcerting, off-putting, and distracting. In addition, it robs you of credibility. Please remember, words matter and tone matters; stay away from emoticons.

You are now ready to participate in a conversation with your community that is local and potentially global and that can help a community think about education in ways that create change. Trust me, the ripple effect can be transforming.

TEACHING AND COMMUNITY LEADERSHIP

If the idea of providing community leadership via a blog is intimidating, remember that excellent teaching is excellent teaching. Approach the blog as you would a classroom because that is virtually what it can and should be.

So what does that mean and what kinds of issues might be addressed?

Keep your eye on the goal of increased understanding. It is so easy to get sidetracked into issues of "the way it should be" or "the way it might be." The goal is about discussion of how a relatively complex system works now; sometimes very well, sometimes a lot less well, and how it might be changed.

Meet your respondents where they are. Do not underestimate their interest. The school is probably a major tax cost in their lives and a major part of their child's life. Do not underestimate their intelligence. They have made lots of decisions and probably recognize the difference between the good, the bad, and the uncertain ones. But, equally, do not underestimate their ignorance. They have neither the time nor the energy to keep up with what is happening. Start at the beginning and bring them up to speed.

Give them the resources to learn. Post the school board minutes; explain where the issues came from and what the implications might be. Bring in outside expertise by making available other useful blogs and Web sites about the issues discussed. More importantly, translate the school budget; where does the money go?

Good questions are better than the best lectures. What are the implications of the board's decisions? What should be the goals of the middle school program? Should we lengthen the school year? What exactly should be the role of a teacher?

Tie the discussions to the local situation. When any topic is discussed bring it down to the doorstep. What do the new state standards mean here; if the student meets this standard could he get a job in town? What would be a better standard? If the state is proposing more, or less, money for education, what does that mean for the local school budget? More important, where should the money come from or go to?

Encourage participants to ask questions and lead the way. Explicitly ask them to tell you what they need or want to know. Their questions are inherently more interesting than yours so make sure they feel free to ask. Their questions are likely to generate more interactions between the participants than yours. This can be expeditionary learning at its best.

Circle back to show patterns and connections. An active blog will zigzag across the terrain of education. It will be easy to forget where you have been. From time to time, you will need to make explicit the connections and, sometimes, the contradictions or conflicts in what has been said and learned.

Several of the above points might be distilled into a short statement of your hopes and expectations for the blog. That statement, with any additions you wish to make, should be at the top of every new post. One such addition might be the rule, a post or response must be true, kind, and get us farther down the road to understanding. This kind of statement is needed because people will come and go from the conversation.

There is one remaining question. If a teacher sets up such a blog, will he be fired? The best guess is no, provided he never breaks one rule. He must never forget that he is not the superintendent or the principal. It is more likely they will be reading the blog regularly. In fact, I do not understand, in this day and age, why they have not either started their own blog or encouraged somebody to do so.

WHAT DOES IT MEAN?

So, what does it mean to be a teacher? In large, complex societies, teachers are responsible for the continuation of the culture. If suddenly all the teachers disappeared, America would soon become not-America. I do not pretend to know what it would become, but whatever it was would not extend from sea to shining sea. Teachers have a huge responsibility both to the present and the future. What they do, or do not do, today will reverberate through society for a long time to come.

The goal of real teaching, not indoctrination, has always been to increase student historicity. To do any less means the death of the American dream. Master teachers are a major counterforce to the increasing disparities of income, opportunity, and mobility that is America today. The form of the counterforce is one of ethics. An unethical master teacher is an oxymoron; such cannot exist. But this is not the ethics of narrowly contrived rules. A master teacher's ethics are the heuristic, existential ethics of variety; a commitment to being fully human and fully alive for both the student and the teacher.

Teaching is never about the generic student somewhere out there. It is about changing the world for the student right in front of you, the one with ambiguous, complex, dynamic, and immediate issues. Teachers have to be creative problem solvers, using whatever options are at hand to deal with often novel and always unique situations. Short of burnout, teaching can never be boring. Every day is going to be different, even for the most experienced teachers who have seen it all before, probably more than once.

Being a master teacher is not an end point; you never get there. It is a continuing journey. The mile markers on the journey are not the usual changes in title, the annual bonus payments, or their ilk. The mile markers are moments of growth and change, the eureka moments of understanding the students, the subject matter, the art and science of teaching, and the self.

Not everyone can, or should, even start on the journey. Please do not even try to be a teacher if you do not have all of the attributes of character: integrity tempered by empathy, intelligence tempered by awe, risk-taking tempered by common sense, independence tempered by ethics, leadership tempered by the desire to serve, and most important, self-confidence tempered by self-knowledge. Even with all the attributes, please do not start or continue on the journey just because it is possible. Start or continue on the journey because it is what you have to do, almost a calling.

It needs that kind of commitment because there are many challenges along the way, even an occasional dragon. What makes a dragon a dragon is any attempt to limit or trivialize another's education for the dragon's selfish reasons. Some challenges may be avoided or circumvented, but dragons must be dealt with as soon as they appear. This means the teacher has to stand up, challenge, and extinguish the flames and smoke produced by a small-brained serpent; be it a student, teacher, parent, administrator, community member, or politician.

If you can stand the occasional flames, teaching is the best career you can have. And if you are a master teacher, nobody can accuse you of just taking up space. "In a completely rational society, the best of us would be teachers and the rest of us would have to settle for something less because passing civilization along from one generation to the next ought to be the highest honor and highest responsibility anyone could have."[5]

NOTES

1. "Reaching All Families: Creating Family-Friendly Schools," 2002. Retrieved March 14, 2008, from http://www.ed.gov/pubs/ReachFam/perscon .html.

2. An introduction to Moodle and a full description can be found at http://moodle.org/.

3. "Internet usage statistics for the Americas (2008)." Retrieved March 14, 2008, from http://www.internetworldstats.com/stats2.htm.

4. D. R. Warlick, *Classroom Blogging; A Teacher's Guide to the Blogosphere* (Raleigh, NC: The Landmark Project, 2005).

5. L. Iacocca, *Where Have All the Leaders Gone?* (New York: Simon & Schuster, 2007), 217.

About the Author

Dexter Chapin has been teaching biology and anthropology for thirty-five years. He has also been a student teacher and a superintendent. Along the way, he has had extraordinary teachers, each of whom changed his life. However, his greatest debt is to his fellow teachers and his students, each of whom opened a door to a new world; a world often beautiful and always complex, uncertain, and on the edge of chaos. How to create a classroom that serves those worlds is the challenge at the core of the teaching profession and the question to which Chapin has dedicated his career.